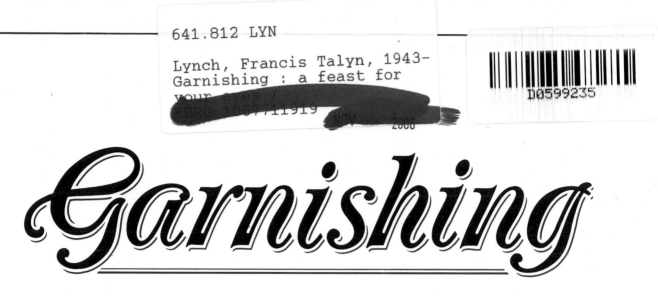

A Feast for Your Eyes

Garnishing

Francis Talyn Lynch

HPBooks

Another Best-Selling Volume from HPBooks

Photography by Myron Beck
Illustrations by Terry Medaris
Food styling for cover and full page photos by Susan Draudt

Published by HPBooks, a division of Price Stern Sloan, Inc.
11150 Olympic Blvd., Suite 650, Los Angeles, CA 90064
©1987 Price Stern Sloan, Inc.
Printed by Dong-A Printing Co., Ltd., Seoul, Korea
Represented by Codra Enterprises, Torrance, California
10 9 8 7 6 5 4

Library of Congress Cataloging in Publication Data

Lynch, Francis Talyn, 1943-
  Garnishing : a feast for your eyes.

  Includes index.
  1. Cookery (Garnishes) I. Title
TX652.L95   1987   641.5   87-8714
ISBN 0-89586-476-2

Contents

Dedication & Acknowledgments

I happily dedicate this book to my loving parents, Al and Irene Lynch, who have always been supportive of me and my "crazy quilt" career.

I also want to acknowledge Bill Sheffield III for encouraging me to dream and to make the dream a reality. For training me to cook and inspiring me to do it well, I am deeply grateful to Chef Etienne Merle, proprietor of L'Auberge du Cochon Rouge, Ithaca, New York. For providing me with the chance to develop my artistry at the many parties we catered together, a special thanks goes to Tom Emery, Valentine Bliss Fine and Michael H. Jones of "A Moveable Feast," Carmel Valley, California. Above all, I'm most grateful to my wonderful wife, Marlinka, for her many hours of proofreading, her very many positive suggestions for clear and enjoyable understanding of my carving instructions and, of course, for her enormous love.

Francis Talyn Lynch started his professional career as a financial analyst even though he grew up in a family that included bakers and restaurateurs. However, after extensive traveling, he succumbed to the lure of the food world. Wanting professional training, he started with a three-year apprenticeship at L'Auberge du Cochon Rouge in Ithaca, New York. Here he became interested in Garde Manger, the art of garnishing. After several years of being a chef in the United States and the Caribbean, he was a partner in an exclusive catering service. Presently he is teaching garnishing in Santa Barbara, where he and his wife Marlinka live. A man of many talents, he works with bronze, stone and wood in addition to sculpting food.

Introduction

Shown are examples of ways to present salads and an appetizer cheese board for a buffet.

DON'T PLAY WITH YOUR FOOD!!! Sound familiar? No doubt you heard those words as a child. Given half a chance, all children do indeed play with food. They draw in it, drum on it and build with it. Still, each generation of children grows up and vainly tries to stifle this very natural form of play in its own offspring—with that famous phrase: "Don't play with your food!"

Well, for the last two or three hundred years, a few kids in each generation have grown up to be a very special breed of professional chef, called *Chefs du Garde Manger*, who are highly respected and sought after *because* they play with food! They draw, sculpt and build with fruit, vegetables and ice, creating the exciting and attractive buffets found in the world's finest clubs and resort hotels.

The purpose of this book is to share with you the special knowledge these chefs use to create their beautiful presentations. Keep in mind they are all simply good cooks who have also learned the basic principles of design and some special cutting techniques. Of course, they work with the very freshest of ingredients, they keep their knives quite sharp and they practice their art, keeping their skills every bit as sharp as their blades. But they're not building rocket ships. Their special knowledge and skills can be learned and mastered by all cooks who want to make their food look as good as it tastes. An old saying goes: "The eyes feast first." Good food that is tastefully arranged and garnished "feeds" our eyes which, in turn, excite our appetites. That is why good cooks always invest a little extra time and attention toward enriching the appearance of their culinary offerings.

When did cooks begin decorating their food? No one really knows. Probably long ago, at the edge of a cave, a flower petal fell onto a bowl of boiled grains. Someone noticed it, liked the way it looked and put a flower or a leaf on another bowl of food soon thereafter. That brief purposeful moment soon passed but the impulse to beautify an offering of food has been developing ever since. Certainly, garnishing has been a global development. It is simply a part of our universally human urge to create beauty. By the early 1700s, the wealthy classes in China, Japan and Western Europe held in highest esteem those chefs who, in addition to being exquisite cooks, exhibited their fares with sculptural and architectural brilliance. They were masters of color, composition and design. In France, banquet tables became so lavish that the upper tiers of food were actually out of reach! Carvings of sugar, ice and tallow (a mixture of animal fat and beeswax) were rendered as pavilions, temples and ancient ruins, and there were all the creatures of the forest, seas and skies to be seen and enjoyed.

Today, buffets are less lavish. Our tastes have become less baroque and few of us can afford to feast in such Lucullan style. Nevertheless, more people today are dining out in clubs, resorts and hotels. It is largely in these establishments that the art of garnishing has been preserved and modernized. In addition, caterers and non-professional, but dedicated, cooks are learning many aspects of this noble culinary art, adding interest and excitement to their tables. Though professionals can certainly use all the ideas in this book, their special facilities and equipment are not needed. The techniques and designs on the following pages are successful because they are based on the natural beauty of food itself. Close attention, sharp knives, quality ingredients and a little (yes, just a little) practice will assure your own success. So relax and . . . play with your food!

What does garnish mean? Actually a garnish can be any edible accent added to a dish. It need not be laid around the dish but may also go onto the food itself. A garnish can be a simple as a sprinkling of paprika or a carrot twist. Garnishes can be a tomato rose in the center of a platter or a row of tomato slices fanned out around the border of a salad bowl. Larger garnishes, like carved cantaloupe ducks or watermelon peacocks, are more properly called *food sculptures* and are used to garnish the table in general. In classical French cuisine the term garnish (*garniture* in French) means all the food on a plate or serving dish other than the meat (or fish or poultry). It was by means of these garnitures that classical French dishes were given their names. Sometimes a name designates a specific food, for example, the term Florentine means that the dish contains spinach; the term Crecy means carrots; du Barry, cauliflower. There is no real logic to the naming of dishes. Chefs do it to honor people, places, dates and historic events. But once the dish is named and defined by its garniture-cum-recipe, it must be prepared with the garnitures that fulfill the name. There are often interesting bits of history attached to classic garnitures.

The dish "Chicken Marengo Sauté" was named after the Battle of Marengo, one of Napoleon's early campaigns. Just before battle, the chef went off to scour the countryside for Napoleon's table. The chef returned with a chicken, garlic, tomatoes, mushrooms, eggs and some crayfish. He sautéed the chicken with these ingredients, frying the eggs separately. Napoleon ate the dish, won the Battle of Marengo and ordered the chef to serve him Chicken Marengo before every battle thereafter. Legend has it, there were no crayfish to be found on the day Napoleon fought—and lost—the Battle of Waterloo! Serving Chicken Marengo without its complete garniture, especially crayfish, has been considered an omen of bad fortune ever since.

GUIDING PRINCIPLES OF VARIETY & CONTRAST

Remember these two important words: *variety* and *contrast*. They are the conceptual corner-stones on which attractive food presentations are based. Without them, you may find yourself serving something like a dish of poached chicken breasts, boiled cauliflower and steamed new potatoes—a plate of white lumps. Good food presentation actually begins with a plan that incorporates foods which, while being gastronomically compatible, differ from one another in color, size, shape and texture. This is not to say, weave a "coat of many colors" every time you compose a plate of food. Do try, however, to create some interest in your dishes via the difference you can establish by adding variety and contrast.

For instance, the "white lump" dish described above could be helped by broiling the chicken to give it color and a crisp skin. The cauliflower might be sauced with a creamed puree of red peppers and the potatoes, sliced, sautéed and sprinkled with a fresh green herb. Now this same set of ingredients has been prepared with a variety of cooking methods, has at least some textural variation, differing shapes and a little color contrast as well. It garnishes itself.

These principles, variety and contrast, are also what make food garnishes and sculptures lively and noticeable. In carving garnishes, one is constantly cutting through food exposing the differences in color, form and texture as they occur naturally in fresh fruit and vegetables. The skin, rind, pulp, flesh and seeds all contrast with one another. Garnishing is a matter of cutting the food, exposing these contrasts, and then rearranging the cut pieces into a new form. This new form can be a simple carrot twist or thin, half slices of tomato arranged in a fan. It can also be a set of V-shaped wedges cut from a melon. These wedges rearranged in a staggered fashion to highlight the color contrasts between rind and flesh, become a wing for a melon swan. That design is particularly powerful because the basic wedges are actually repetitions of the same form, an arc. Repetition plays an important role in attention-getting garnishes.

Nature uses repetition of line and form to create its attractive designs. A daisy is really a pattern wherein the same part, the petal, is repeated over and over; each petal radiates out of the center of the daisy, just like the one next to it, filling all the space around the center. This repetition can be found throughout nature: in the scales of fish, feathers on birds, crystals in snowflakes and in artificial designs like shingles on a roof, spokes in a wheel and rungs of a ladder. Patterns generally repeat the same or similar lines. Interestingly, all patterns are composed of only two kinds of lines: straight or curved. These two kinds of lines, in turn, can have only one of two possible actions—they either run parallel to each other or they angle toward one another, eventually meeting.

So what? Well knowing this makes the understanding of what you'll be doing with your knives as you cut your garnishes a lot simpler. You see, your knives are already straight, so it really isn't too hard to cut a straight slice. That takes care of half of all possible lines. The other half is largely taken care of by the food itself, because most foods are round or somewhat so. Therefore the other kind of lines, the curved ones, are nature's gift. This is why fruit and vegetable carving expertise is so common among professional chefs: they may not be artistic enough to draw a duck but, with a sharp knife and a fresh apple, they can carve a delightful apple duck as a centerpiece for an hors d'oeuvre platter—and so can you!

SERVING DISHES

Gold is the only metal that is completely safe to serve food from. All other metals will react with one food or another. Stainless steel is the next best choice, but it does react with recipes containing egg yolks, turning them green and is not recommended as a material in which to serve marinades. Aluminum platters will turn marinades iridescent and aluminum pots make light wine-based sauces turn grey. In an aluminum roasting pan, I once marinated 40 pounds of beef steaks in a lovely red wine and rosemary bath. The next morning I had 40 pounds of green steaks to explain away to my boss, who was not Irish enough to see the beauty in the event. On the following payday my pay envelope was a bit short of the old green stuff—about 40 steaks worth.

Silver tarnishes in contact with egg whites and should not be used to hold highly acidic or alkaline foods for more than an hour, lest any silver oxide wash off into your food. Copper is highly reactive and should not be used to serve moist foods. Pewter contains lead and should be used only as a container for dry foods, if at all. Dishes lined with tin are safe but are likely to impart a metallic taste to acidic marinades. Tin often covers copper, so be sure the tin plating is in good repair. Well seasoned cast iron pots are safe for most hot foods.

Serving dishes made from wood, glass, crystal, ceramic, stone, lacquerware and plastic are safe. Larger foods like melons and banana squash can also be used as serving vessels. If you use the reactive metal serving platters, first lay down a buffer of romaine or red Swiss chard leaves to protect cold food. Use crackers, pastry shells or toast points to buffer hot and cold foods.

Professional chefs often coat their metallic serving platters with layers of aspic or other gelatin-based sauces. When cooled and hardened these sauces serve as highly attractive buffers on which to serve cold foods; see pages 135-137.

SIZES & SHAPES

Serving dishes come in five basic shapes: square, rectangular, round, oval and faceted. Deep-dished bowls have sides that are round, flared or straight up and down. A few common-sense guidelines will help in arranging food in these vessels so they are attractive and easy to serve from.

1. Fill deep-dished bowls above the level of the rim, that is, mound the food. Shape the mound, if possible, then decorate the shape. These shapes can be simple round domes or domes with flat tops, diamonds, cubes, pyramids and shapes that rise in steps. Whatever shape the mound takes, its base should begin to move in from the edge of the bowl about an inch below the rim. This space inside the rim can be left empty or partially filled with bite-size garnishes. All garnishes intended for consumption should be bite-size.

2. Any food used as a border or as part of a design laid onto the surface of your food should be one of the ingredients of the dish itself, or at least be very complimentary to it.

3. Foods look larger and more striking when framed in a complete border. However, a partial border going around the back of the dish, serving as a crown, will work almost as well.

4. Use the flat rims of *platters* as space on which to lay a border of thinly sliced foods—circles, herringbone, half-circles and

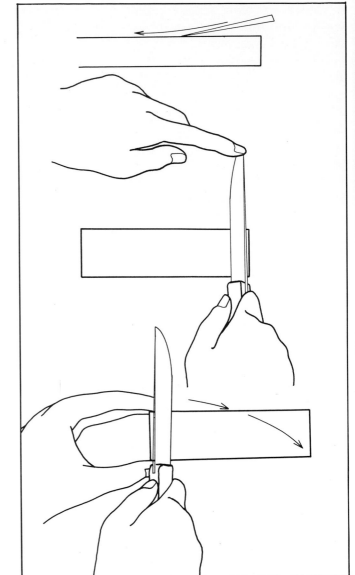

points. Traditionally, it is considered bad form to decorate the rims of *individual plates*.

KNIVES

The key to successful garnishing is a sharp knife. A sharp knife does not need to be pushed or forced, and it enables you to maintain control of the depth and direction of your cuts—and your temper. Well meaning cooks have shown up at my garnishing classes with everything from grapefruit knives to blades designed to cut through blocks of frozen food. So far no one has come in with an electric knife, a device I feel is

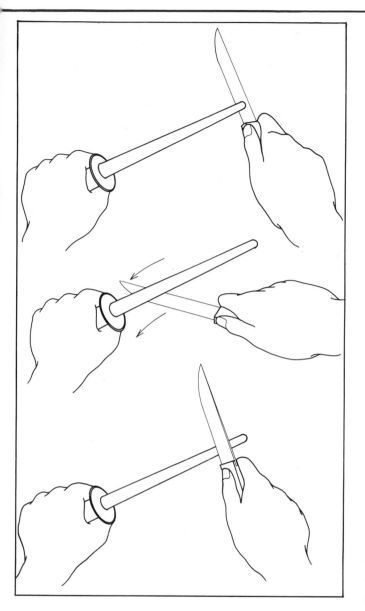

best. The shiny supermarket knife is too flexible, too light and too hard to sharpen.

All three knives are kept sharp in exactly the same way. You first create a sharp cutting edge by stroking the blade across a flat, abrasive stone, then smooth this sharp edge on a metal or ceramic rod, called a *steel*. You may want to have your knives professionally sharpened and then use a steel to keep them in good condition. Cutlery stores perform this sharpening service, and their rates are quite low. Whether you sharpen the knives yourself, or not, you will need a steel.

To do your own sharpening, buy a six- to eight-inch stone that has one coarse side and one very smooth side. The coarse side is used to grind down chips in the blade. Most actual sharpening is done on the fine surface. Lay the stone on a rag so it won't slip. Generously wet the stone with plain mineral oil; you don't need fancy, expensive oils. Salad oils will eventually turn gummy, so avoid them. **Now, just in front of the knife handle, lay the cutting edge of the blade on one end of the stone. (Imagine you are trying to shave off the top of the stone, the whole stone, with the whole knife.) The cutting edge of the blade should be facing down the length of the stone and held at a very low angle—no more than 20 degrees. Place the fingers of your free hand near the end of the blade, and keep them there to steady the blade through each stroke. Pass the cutting edge of the knife all along the entire length of the stone. As you do this, draw the knife closer to you so the entire length of the blade has been drawn over the stone by the end of the pass. Now reverse the action, laying the other side of the blade against the stone and pass it along the stone in the opposite direction. Repeat this process of shaving the stone back and forth 20 to 30 times. Remember to hold the knife at a very, very low angle. The lower the angle, the sharper your knife will be.**

The steel you use should have a fine, almost smooth, surface. The action on the steel is much like that used on the stone. **Hold the steel in your free hand and pass your knife down the length of the steel at a low angle, in the**

somehow related to a paper shredder in terms of control and finesse. You'll need three good knives for the designs in this book: a small paring knife, a medium-size knife with a six-inch blade and a large knife with a nine- or ten-inch blade. Do not use serrated knives. These are beveled (angled) on only one side of the blade and will veer off in the direction of the bevel.

Top-quality knives are recommended. They are expensive, but they're strong, have excellent balance, sharpen easily and will last a lifetime. Blades made of high-carbon stainless steel are direction of the knife's cutting edge. Make one full stroke with one side of the blade against the steel. With each step the entire length of the blade should be drawn into contact with the steel. A repetition of light, alternating strokes works best. Quick, flashy strokes are ineffective. There are two recommended positions for holding the steel. The safest way is to hold the tip of the steel pointing straight down, resting on a cloth on your cutting board. This position forces you to stroke away from your body. However, the classic position puts the steel out in front of your chest, tip up and tilted, so that the rod bisects the angle between your head and shoulder. If you're right handed, the tip is sloping to the right; left handed, to the left.

CLASSICAL CUTS

Many recipes designate a particular cut of food. These are usually small sticks and cubes. They add a crisp geometric look to the finished dish, imparting a sense of care and precision to your presentations.

To cut precise shapes efficiently, first slice the food into a square or rectangular block. When slicing, be sure to hold your blade pointed down at a 45 degree angle so that as little of the blade as possible actually contacts the food. This reduces the tendency of the food to cling to the knife. You want to keep the food in a neat stack as you cut. Use the fingers of your free hand to keep the food in place.

First cut the food in slices of the desired width. Then cut these again, creating the desired depth. Now cut across the stack to the desired length.

SPECIALTY TOOLS

In addition to the three standard knives, you will be using a vegetable peeler. The standard one with a blade that swivels works best. The marketplace is full of expensive models, but the ordinary supermarket variety is recommended. Definitely avoid a peeler that does not swivel; this design digs too deeply into the food. Strangely enough, these stiff peelers are often labelled *gourmet* peeler. That's a bit like calling a

hatchet a gourmet cleaver.

Oriental markets and some gourmet cookware stores sell small punches, which work like cookie cutters but are much stronger. They are used to punch shapes out of vegetables and can be used on cured meats and firm cheeses as well. Professional chefs use another type of shaped punch called aspic cutters. Their purpose is to cut sheets of colored gelatin or very thin slices of food. Aspic cutters are rather delicate, small tools but like the Oriental vegetable punches, can be used to create special accents for salads, soups, dinner plates, hors d'oeuvre platters and cold meat or cheese trays.

In general, avoid multi-purpose kitchen tools. They don't work. If you want a specialty garnishing tool, treat yourself to a good product. Go for quality.

Zester & Citrus Scorer

Many simple and effective garnishing effects are achieved with two special knives: a zester and a scorer. These tools are inexpensive and highly recommended. The zester and the citrus scorer (also called a stripper) are two unusual knives used by chefs to create color and texture contrasts on the surface of foods. In addition to the following uses described below, the zester and scorer can be used to texture the sides of melon birds, vegetable vases, watermelon baskets and the hull of the radish sailboat. I strongly recommend two specific brands for these tools. For a zester, try to find the Victorinox model. For a scorer, try to find one made by Econome Inox.

Zest is another name for the colorful, aromatic skin of citrus fruit. A zester cuts this shallow layer of skin away from the fruit in thin threads. A well-designed zester has a rigid, rectangular "blade," 3 inches long and 1/2 inch wide. The end of the blade is bent down about 30 degrees and this bent end is perforated by a row of very small holes. To use it, you hold the bent end angled down against the food and pull the zester into the food. It instantly takes a bite through the small holes. Then you simply pull it along the surface, cutting out threads of skin and leaving a pattern of parallel grooves behind.

Drawing the zester down the length of a zucchini or cucumber before slicing them gives the slices an attractive striped appearance. The zester is also used to shred a carrot into threads which are then used as borders for salads. A single layer zested from a carrot gives the carrot an unusual spiky surface so any crosscut slices cut from it will look more exciting. Of course, the zester cuts delicate threads from lemons, limes and oranges. These threads are used in various recipes, and can be tied in simple knots, poached a few minutes in simple syrup, then used as elegant garnishes for desserts.

The scorer cuts one single strip of skin at a time. This strip is about a quarter-inch wide and an eighth-inch deep. There are scorers for right-handed cooks and left-handed cooks. These pull toward your thumb. There's also a type which pulls toward the handle and it can be used by all, though generally, the ones that pull to the side are easier to control. The blade of a scorer is a small U-shaped loop lying under a flat tongue of metal, which, in turn, sticks out of the handle. Some scorers have large loops. Avoid these; they cut too deeply.

You can use the scorer alone or with a zester. For instance, you can score horizontal strips from a whole lemon, then cut the lemon into wedges. Each wedge will have yellow and white stripes. Another variation calls for partially scoring strips down the sides of a lemon. Leave the strips attached at the bottom by sliding the scorer back up, unthreading each strip. To serve, tuck the strip under itself to form a loop. Slip a little sprig of parsley or other herb into the loop.

Scored fruit and vegetable strips can be tied in bows. Cut two strips, each six inches long. Hold each strip in a loop. Pass the ends of the right loop through the left, then bend the ends of the left loop through the right loop. Gently pull the ends apart, tightening the loops into a bow. Trim the ends as desired.

By the way, all lemon wedges can be brightened by dipping the narrow, straight edges into chopped (or dried) herbs or spices. If you are laying out whole slices as garnishes, first score the whole lemon lengthwise, then

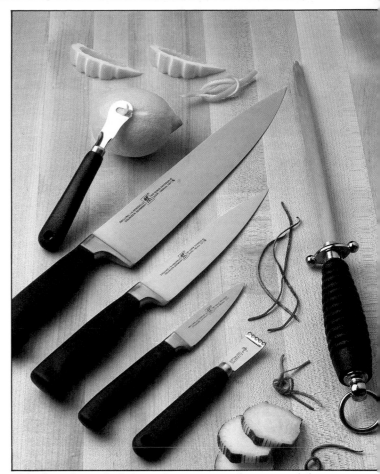

This photo shows the knives, citrus scorer and zester needed to make the designs in this book.

slice it. Now, lay the slices along the front of your cutting board. One at a time, lay a teaspoon upside down onto the slice and dust paprika around the spoon. The paprika will soon darken. To serve, place a small herb leaf into the undusted space.

DINNER PLATE

An attractive dinner plate begins with properly cooked food. No amount of garnishing will improve the grey look of an overcooked dinner. Who wants to sit down to a fish fillet that resembles a pile of puzzle parts? What garnish could possibly put it right? None. Therefore, begin by cooking correctly. Finish by arranging your well cooked food with care. Then, any extra garnish you care to add to the plate can (and should) be quite simple. Think of the dinner plate garnish as a beauty mark on an already attractive face.

Plate garnishes can be a sprinkling of a Brunoise (cut into dice 1/16th inch wide) of carrot over the green beans. Your garnish may be a bit of fresh herb, such as parsley, dill, thyme, sage, oregano, rosemary, chives and cilantro. The vegetable twists, bows and knots are perfect dinner place accents. So are turned mushrooms and small green onion ferns. See page 13 for some variations of the common lemon wedge. You may want to go as far as to put a three-sectioned wing (page 54) cut from a suitable fruit or vegetable on the plate, but by and large, keep the plate garnish simple. Let the actual food be its own primary garnish.

To arrange food so it does garnish itself, remember the principles of variety and contrast. Use foods of different sizes, shapes, textures and colors. Do not crowd the plate. Leave some space around each item, not too much, just a small frame. Let each item contrast with its background and stand apart on its own stage, so to speak. If you have the traditional meat, starch and vegetable composition for your dinner, avoid serving three whole chunks: a whole steak, whole baked potato and a single clump of cauliflower or broccoli. Slice the potato into batons or diamonds, then oven-fry these pieces. Serve the cauliflower in smaller flowerets arranged in a row or half-circle. Easier yet, begin your dinner with an eye toward its final look and substitute a colored pasta, wild rice mix or even plain rice for the potato. Select a vegetable with a naturally different shape to begin with, such as peas, asparagus or green beans, and you're way ahead from the start.

Assuming that the items on the dinner plate have been well selected, properly cooked and tastefully arranged, only one thing can go wrong. And unfortunately it does all too often. What is it? Over saucing! A veritable blanket of opaque gravy is, in a well-meaning effort to make sure everyone gets a generous portion, thickly poured over at least the main ingredient on the plate and possibly more.

Sauces and gravies are meant to enhance the flavor of food, not obscure it. Just so, as a visual accent, the sauce should be laddled on in a way that still allows the diner to see the food being sauced. Thick sauces are laid over the food in a ribbon. Thin sauces can be more generously applied as they will run off and leave the food visible, though finely glazed. If needed, extra sauce is served on the table in a sauce boat.

Another approach is to first lay the sauce down on the plate and place the food into the center of it, letting the sauce frame the food from below. This popular and attractive technique is called under saucing. It can be very striking when two sauces are used. Of course, the sauces should compliment each other and be about the same thickness, though of different colors: a combination of white beurre blanc and brown demi-glace for instance. Thinned purees of vegetables can be employed as sauces, too, thus broadening the color palette considerably. An extreme example of artful undersaucing is accomplished by completely covering the plate with a thin layer of sauce. The meat is then placed into the sauce and small drops of the second sauce are carefully placed around the meat or just inside the rim of the plate. These drops are applied with a paper pastry bag or a plastic squeeze bottle fitted with a nozzle. The drops can be left alone in their elegant simplicity or swirled around with the point of a knife. Any vegetables or starches are served on a side dish.

COMPOSED SALADS

The expression "composing a salad" describes a very artistic, well-planned approach to making up a salad plate characterized by a definite, recognizable pattern. The pattern is usually geometric: a star, wagon wheel, sunburst, fan or compass design. In addition, natural forms like flowers, birds, butterflies, trees and masks or faces can be fashioned through the careful placement of your salad ingredients.

In addition to the extra time needed to make up composed salads, extra refrigeration space is likewise required. Nevertheless, composed salads are a delight to serve and should be included on menus for special, small parties. One Palm Sunday some years back, I was catering a brunch for a well-heeled family in San Francisco. They had an enormous kitchen and I needed every single inch of it to lay out 100 composed fruit salads each in the shape of a palm tree. Had I been anywhere else, I would have completely arrested the preparation of the remainder of the menu. Oh, the salads were a big hit, but I was definitely less than one in the eyes of my fellow cooks whose preparations had to slow down while I finished the palms.

The key to composing a salad is in being organized. First, of course, have a design. Sketch it out. Then, try it out once. When you have composed one salad to your satisfaction, then go about cutting each ingredient until all the components have been neatly cut and set into separate stacks. Lay your plates out in one or more rows and begin the laying on of the food. Go from plate to plate placing one item down at a time. Then proceed with the next item. Remember, you are basically working backwards—building up the background first.

In developing your designs, allow yourself the freedom of building a little height to your salad. Star-cut stuffed tomatoes and stuffed avocado halves both accomplish this nicely. A hollowed out 3-inch cucumber section can be set on end and filled with strips of crisp vegetables for an unusual, yet pleasant, salad. A lattice of vegetables, such as a hearts of palm salad, can be built up a few inches on the plate.

If your salad dressing is thick and creamy, don't apply it. Place the dressing on the table in a separate sauce boat. You don't want to hide your design under a coat of thick dressing. Thin, clear dressings can be carefully ladled on just before serving.

SOUPS

Clear, thin soup, called consomme or bouillon, requires only the slightest amount of garnish. Typically, the items used are foods which have been cut into very small pieces in the shape of cubes, diamonds or matchsticks. Special shapes cut with aspic cutters are also suitable. Five or six pieces are sufficient for each serving. They will not float, so a large number of garnishes would simply sink into a mysterious pile at the bottom of the bowl.

What should you choose as a specific garnish for a particular consomme? Let your recipe guide you. Obviously, flaked salmon would not be used to garnish a beef bouillon. Slivers of mushroom would be far more palatable. Small leaves of fresh herbs, cut and blanched vegetables, cooked or cured meats, truffles, custards and julienned crepes are all appropriate embellishments. Be sure your garnishes are not raw (except fresh herbs) and they should be hot before going into the servings.

Creamed soups are usually thick enough to support a few lightweight slices of food on their surfaces. These slices should be quite thin and carefully laid on one at a time. Thick vegetable purees will support a relatively broad (but bite-sized) slice of the vegetable from which they are made. Certainly all creamed soups can be dusted with a spice, such as curry powder, nutmeg or paprika. Herbs, if used, are best when fresh; a single leaf or flower is enough. Liquids can also be used to create an inviting color and taste contrast. Ladle a tablespoon of heavy cream, vegetable puree or even a meat sauce into the center of each serving.

Adding garnishes to stew-like soups such as minestrone is uncalled for. Stay with small croutons if you do wish to float something on these hearty dishes.

PASTRY BAGS

The pastry bag, which is also called a forcing bag, can be used for far more than applying icings to cakes. In the realm of desserts, the pastry bag is used to make meringue shells, pipe eclairs and cream puffs, top a variety of desserts with whipped cream, fill vessels with mousse and draw with chocolate, to name but a few of its diverse functions. As an aid in general cooking, the pastry bag enables one to draw with sauces, pipe whipped potatoes and vegetable purees into borders and individual servings, create butter roses and stars, fill devilled eggs and vegetable canapes with an array of cheese, fish and meat purees or pâtés.

Because pastry bags can be used with an assortment of tips that form stars, straight lines, scalloped patterns, leaves and flower petals, they are an important addition to the tool kit of cooks who wish to present their culinary offerings with artistic flair. A piped turban of mashed potatoes, passed in a hot oven to color, is certainly more appetizing than a plain spooned-on dollop of pale potato. A butter dish containing individual butter stars or scallop shells is far more pleasing than the standard quarter-pound block.

Pastry bags (and an enormous assortment of tips) are readily available at good cookware stores. They are made of plastic or rubber-coated cloth and, when opened, look like cones. It's a good idea to have a few of these commercial bags on hand because hand-made bags aren't sufficiently strong enough to pipe very dense foods. It is an equally good idea to be able to make your own bag out of parchment paper (also available at cookware stores) because some foods, such as chocolate, purees of beet, carrot, pimiento and mousses of blueberry, raspberry or coffee, can stain the cloth bags and then possibly taint the next food piped through with an unwanted color.

CHEESE SERVICE

There are two broad categories of cheese service: hors d'oeuvre cheese service and sliced cheese intended to become part of a sandwich. The latter category can be treated very much like cold cuts of meat. Arrange sliced cheese platters by carefully laying down the slices, one at a time, forming neat rows which may be straight and parallel or converging; or lay the rows out in swirls, serpentines, semicircles and full circles. Don't lay cheese slices onto lettuce leaves. The moisture in the leaves will ruin the cheese's color and texture. Use two colors of cheese slices to create more striking patterns, using corners and edges of the slices to define the pattern. See the photograph on the opposite page for an example of this.

Hors d'oeuvre cheeses should be served on wooden boards or marble slabs. If the mesh is small and tight, wicker trays are also serviceable, though hard to clean. A variety of cheese is suggested for broadening the appeal of this hors d'oeuvre. For instance, a blue-veined Roquefort, a semi-soft Bel Paese and an aged Cheddar make up a balanced, yet varied, presentation. Because the soft, ripe family of cheese to which Brie, Camembert and the Double and Triple Creams belong tends to ooze somewhat, it's best to serve these on their own separate board. All cheese in this hors d'oeuvre group should be allowed to warm up outside the refrigerator for at least a half hour.

By virtue of their varied shapes, colors and textures cheeses are naturally inbued with eye appeal. Arrange your hors d'oeuvre cheese trays using a wedge shape, a cylinder, a ball, a wheel, or punch out small shapes of the aged cheeses (Swiss and Cheddar) with aspic or vegetable cutters. These punched shapes can be skewered along with seedless grapes and served individually as well.

Fruit, of course, is the preferred food group with which to garnish cheese. If you serve grapes, first snip the larger cluster into mini-clusters of three or four grapes, then use these to reconstruct the larger cluster on your presentation board. Try to use seedless grapes.

Slices of apple (quickly dipped in fresh lemon juice to keep them white), apricots, pears (if cut immediately before serving), figs, plums, peaches and strawberries can be arrayed in attractive spirals and fans in the corners of the cheese board. Apple birds, small melon birds, the kiwifruit songbird and pear quail are all appropriate sculptures for cheese presentations.

PRESENTATION OF HOT & COLD MEATS
Hot Meats

Freshly roasted meats are served sliced and arranged on serving platters, or left whole and carved during service. Either way, garnishes are best kept simple. An elaborate garnish would detract from the natural beauty of the meat (fish or fowl) but, more importantly, simply be in the

Shown here are suggestions for arranging meat and cheese for sandwiches.

way of the person serving and carving. A border of halved cranberries surrounding the platter of sliced turkey, for instance, will frame and attractively set off a holiday platter. Skillet-browned whole pearl onions and baby carrots will garnish a warm tray of roast beef. Fresh herbs are always appropriate.

When carving meat in front of your guests, use a cutting board that has a groove in its surface to catch any excess juices. It is advisable to let any roast rest outside the oven for at least ten minutes before carving. This will allow the juices to stop flowing and resettle into the meat. The roast will be tastier and you will lose less juice when you carve. Cutting boards are usually roomy enough to permit placing a carved garnish in at least one corner, and a border of sliced vegetables around the sides. The garnish can be a bouquet of tomato roses framed with parsley, other vegetable flowers, turned mushrooms, an apple duck, pear quail or Daikon butterfly. Place these small sculptures out in front, but on the opposite side from which you're carving the roast.

Cold Meats

There is no great secret or short cut to making up cold meat presentations. It is simply a matter of laying out slices of meat as if you were dealing out a deck of cards: you do it one slice at a time. Use a wooden carving board, metal tray, lacquerware dish, mirror or glass platter. All are flat and will permit the use of a small sculpture or vegetable flower as garnish. The primary garnish, however, is a neat arrangement of the meat slices in rows that form an attractive pattern. These patterns can be straight rows or curving serpentines, spirals, wagon wheels or sunbursts. If your tray is small, relative to the quantity of meat you are serving, roll the slices into cylinders or cones before arranging them. Rolled slices use less surface area and add height to your presentation. See page 17 for examples of this.

If you are serving cold roasts or a pâté, save a whole section of the meat and display it along with the slices to add authenticity and mass to your presentation. For cold cuts, use some slices

to fashion a flower as a focal point.

Cold meats are also satisfyingly garnished with naturally tart or pickled foods, such as olives, pepperoncini, cornichons, marinated vegetables, artichoke hearts and small onions. Pork loins, ham and prosciutto are traditionally accompanied by succulent fruits, such as pineapple, melons and papaya.

Smoked salmon is usually served with plain or herb-flavored cream cheese. Arrange your slices so they form the shape of a salmon, then pipe the creamed cheese around your fish using a pastry bag. At holiday time, cut the salmon into triangular slices and layer them in the shape of a Christmas tree. Use a small bit of cream cheese for the tree trunk. In the summer, cut the slices into crescents and lay them out forming the circular shape of a palm tree. Again, use cream cheese to form a tall, tubular tree trunk. When you make these trees, begin your designs by laying down the outermost branches first. Make a complete pattern and then keep adding layers until the trees have a pleasing three-dimensional appearance.

Be sure, of course, that you offer a cold meat your guests will appreciate. I once served oak-smoked salmon at a party largely attended by a group of young athletes whose palates had barely experienced bologna. They ate the bread. They ate the cream cheese, and they completely ignored my salmon cypress tree!

Avoid using small cocktail forks as serving utensils for cold meats. Ice tongs or a broad, flat serving fork work much better. Also lay out a small butter knife for the cream cheese or other spread, and do have a basket of small bread slices right next to the cold meat presentation.

CRUDITÉS & ANTIPASTO PLATTERS

Crisp, colorful fresh vegetables are a healthy and deservedly popular hors d'oeuvre called *crudités* (pronounced kroo dee tays). The word literally means raw and indeed most of the time this is the state in which these vegetables are served. Occasionally large asparagus is first blanched 30 seconds or broccoli flowerets 10 seconds to brighten and tenderize them. In all cases the vegetables are cut into finger-food sizes of various shapes: sticks, rounds, ovals or flowerets. Solid vegetables such as turnips, Daikon radishes and jicama can be cut into special shapes with the vegetable punches and aspic cutters.

Vegetables enjoyed by most people are carrots, celery, cucumbers, zucchini, red and Daikon radishes, summer squash, cherry tomatoes, red, green and yellow bell peppers, green onions, turnips, broccoli, cauliflower, asparagus, Belgian endive, young green beans, snow peas and fennel. Though not a vegetable, raw mushrooms are also served as a crudité. Use your zester and citrus stripper to create novel color contrasts down and around the sides of cucumbers and zucchini before cutting them into round slices, diagonally cut ovals or sticks. A corrugated knife known as a *krinkle cutter* will make waffled sides and edges on foods cut with it. Keep your cut vegetables wrapped in wet paper towelling and sealed in plastic bags if you slice them up a day or two ahead. Don't soak them in water for it ruins their taste and nutritional value.

Dipping sauces for crudités should be thick enough to cling to the food. Sauces may be served from small bowls, large bell peppers, hollowed Table Queen or Hubbard squash and hollowed heads of red, green or Savoy cabbage.

Crudités are served on flat platters or in wicker baskets or shallow bowls. See photo page 61. When making up an arrangement in a bowl or basket, line the bottom with enough fresh leafy material to lift your crudités up so they show above the rim. Romaine leaves; curly endive (chicory); red, white or green kale; red Swiss chard or savoy cabbage all serve this purpose well. The actual arrangement depends, of course, on the vegetables you have to work with. Whatever they are, lay them out in bundles, rows and stacks so that each item is noticeable and contrasts in color with its immediate neighbor.

On flat platters use the various colors and shapes you have to create a geometric pattern. This can be as simple as parallel rows, a sunburst or a wagon wheel. Use smaller items like red radishes, cherry tomatoes and broccoli

flowerets to make borders between and around the segments of your pattern. The use of leafy underliners is by no means a necessity and can make a precise pattern difficult to achieve. If you do use a leafy underliner, press the spines of the leaves flat to minimize their potential interference with your design. Crudité baskets and platters can be garnished with tomato roses, green onions, carrot, radish and chili flowers, Daikon butterflies, turned mushrooms and various vegetable twists.

Highly spiced and usually marinated, the flavorful foods that fall under the heading of *antipasto* have become very welcome additions to hors d'oeuvre menus. Because they are so strongly flavored, these vegetables are not served on the same dish as the more lightly flavored crudités. However, the principles which govern their arrangement are the same as for flat platters of crudités except the dish should be non-metallic.

Pepperoncini, ripe and green olives, pickled cauliflower, carrots, green beans and celery as well as marinated mushrooms and cherry peppers are all excellent for antipasto. In addition, sardines, anchovies, pepperoni, salami and prosciutto will please antipasto lovers. Place a small bouquet of salami flowers (page 37) on your antipasto platter for garnish. Tomato roses, chili flowers and turned mushrooms are also appropriate.

THE BUFFET TABLE

You can avoid a flat looking buffet by elevating some of your dishes, food sculptures and certainly your centerpiece with simple pedestals covered with extra linen. These pedestals can be made with wood or styrofoam blocks, inverted baking pans and small boxes. Footed cake servers and tiered hors d'oeuvre trays also add height to your table. The centerpiece can be even higher than eye level but it is generally at or just below that height. Try to achieve a balance of heights on the left and the right of the centerpiece.

If both cold and hot foods are being served on the same table, the cold items are set out at the beginning of the buffet. Use serving utensils that will allow your guests to conveniently serve themselves with one hand, such as tongs and oversized spoons and forks. If your guests are picking up their own silverware from the buffet, wrap each set in a napkin and place these sets in fans or stacks at the end of the buffet.

Place your serving dishes in from the front of the buffet by six inches or so. This will prevent most spills from falling onto the floor and help keep peoples' clothing from rubbing into the food. If your table looks too sparse, fill in some of the empty space with runners of ivy, ferns, kale, chicory or evergreen boughs, and place vegetable flowers along the runners.

When you have a special party theme or are featuring a particular ethnic cuisine, dress your table with linens, cooking utensils and some of the raw ingredients found in your menu. A Mexican fiesta theme, for instance, calls for fresh and dried chilies, serpentines of pinto beans and rice, corn husks and long cinnamon sticks. Non-edible props like *sombreros*, *serapes* and small *piñatas* would strongly support the Mexican theme, too. For an Oriental party, you might serve some food in woks, bamboo trays, laquerware and porcelain china. Paper lanterns, fans and bundles of chopsticks tied in silk scarves and set upright are simple but effective props used to enhance an Oriental theme. How about Western? Checkered linen, white and blue speckled platters and bowls, cast iron kettles and pots, polished spurs and new horseshoes would certainly make a strong Western statement. Rows of whole oats and wheat, fresh corn and dried beans surrounding your dishes would add extra Western flavor. Looking around for props will take you to stores and locales you might not otherwise visit. It takes some extra time but it's educational, makes for an unusual date, and adds authenticity and excitement to your party.

TIPS FOR WATERMELON BASKETS

1. Select a firm melon with a solid, low-pitched sound when tapped with your knuckle. A high pitch indicates extreme water pressure within melon, which means melon will probably split when you cut into it. Of course, if

you can't tell a high note from a foghorn, this advice won't help a bit. Just follow step two.

2. Be sure melon is at room temperature before cutting it.

3. Take bottom (or side depending on design) off with a straight, single slice using a large chef's knife.

4. You may want to draw your design onto melon first. Use a felt tipped, "dry-erase" marker, which wipes very easily.

5. Begin cutting of all watermelon baskets and sculptures with just very tip of paring knife. Etch entire design into surface of melon no more than 1/4 inch deep.

6. After etching, go back over design with your paring knife, cutting 1 inch deep. As you cut into melon, always have your blade aiming into its core (center line). Cut with a sawing motion.

7. Now sink your cuts well into melon with a 6-inch knife. Cut areas of melon to be removed into small sections, then pull them out one section at a time.

8. Cut *inside* of walls and handles with your knife so they will have smooth sides. Then scoop out center with a serving spoon.

9. If wrapped and refrigerated, cut melons last four days. Designs with long thin handles tend to droop a bit after two days.

10. When carving handles into baskets, cut them with their details, such as, waves, scallops, etc. However, it is easier to cut edges of basket itself in straight lines and then go back and add details. If you wait to trim handles when they have no support from melon body, they often break.

SECRETS FOR SUCCESSFUL FOOD SCULPTURING

First things first. Your workspace is going to affect all you try to accomplish as a food sculptor, so set up a work station in your kitchen that enables you to function comfortably and efficiently. If you can manage to sit and work at a table, then by all means do so. Some cooks are so used to standing while they work that sitting down throws their sense of comfort and control out of kilter. Whether you sit or stand, avoid bending over and into your work. Your back won't take being bent over for long. If you are standing, use a footpad. A doormat cushions your feet well, is inexpensive and can be put back outside when you're finished. If your cutting board slides out, pull it out of its slot and lay it on top of your counter. This raises its height 2 to 4 inches—important inches that will stand you up straight as you work. If the board tends to slip around, just moisten a cloth, lay it out flat and let your board rest on it. The cloth will anchor the board.

Some of the cutting is quite precise. Avoid eye strain by placing a bright reading lamp to your right, if you are right-handed; to the left if you're left-handed. A lamp with a flexible neck, the standard desk-top design, will do the job.

Controlling Knife Strokes

If you skipped the section on knife sharpening (page 11) please go back to it. YOUR KNIVES MUST BE VERY SHARP.

Okay. Now your knives are sharp and you're ready to go. Here's some great news: there are only two major cutting techniques to learn, and you probably do a variation of one of them already. The first technique is the *saw cut* which is the action used in slicing fresh bread. This saw cut is used over and over again in a variety of directions and with both long and short strokes. For example, you'll find yourself sawing your way around a tomato when carving a tomato rose and you'll be sawing into apples and melons to make the wings for apple ducks and melon swans. The saw cut is characterized by a soft downward pressure (going in the direction of the cutting edge of your blade) that never fully lets up. That is, when your knife comes to a stop at the end of a stroke you avoid any lifting of your hand or wrist, thus keeping the cutting edge fully seated in the very bottom of the cut at all times. Another important aspect of the saw cut is aiming the direction of the cut by sighting across the center of the middle of the blade; that is you work with your knife so the blade is at, or very near, a right angle to the direction of your cut. Another way of saying this is: Don't dip the tip of your knife up or

down. The saw cut may feel inefficient at first because you are used to cutting food quickly for cooking, as in slicing onions, and a heavy touch has always made the work go faster. In food sculpting, speed is secondary to control. Switch to an exaggerated sawing motion with a steady, LIGHT PRESSURE and, thus, control your cuts. Note that the surfaces of foods are often tougher than the flesh underneath, so be sure to use a light touch on those first few strokes, too.

The other frequently used cut is called the *pencil stroke*. It is used to draw designs and make shallow cuts. You'll find it useful when tracing the birds' heads patterns on pages 139-141. The pencil stroke is also employed as the primary cutting action for short straight lines. It's called a pencil stroke because you grip the blade of a paring knife between the tips of your thumb and first two fingers just like you'd hold a pencil. Sometimes you may find it more efficient to hold the paring knife by its handle and use a stroke that imitates a house painter's downward brush stroke. Either way, the cut is characterized by penetrating the surface of the food to a very precise, shallow depth, then drawing the tip of the blade along the surface in a continuous line, using no sawing motion whatsoever and thus carving a nice, clean line. Obviously, if the tip of your knife is dull, or even slightly bent, your work will be very hard to control. You will be exerting too much force in compensating for the shortcomings of your blade, thereby losing the smooth, deliberate motion otherwise provided by the pencil stroke.

Fastening

Quite often you will be attaching one piece of food to another, securing the head of an apple turkey to its body, for instance. The food sculptor's glue comes in the form of wooden picks and skewers. Use two wooden picks (or skewers) whenever possible. One alone tends to create a hinge or swivel on which one piece of food will tend to spin or droop. Also, be sure your wooden picks are fairly parallel for if they aren't, you will be setting up a little wooden spring that will push the pieces of your sculpture apart.

Avoid dyed wooden picks. They are not colorfast. Also avoid wooden picks whose shafts are round. Some brands are called round but their shafts have four flat sides and it is the flat-sided style of pick you want to use. It is stronger and much easier to control for they won't roll around on your cutting board.

Wooden (usually bamboo) skewers come in lengths up to 12 inches. The short ones are thin but are still stronger than wooden picks. It's good to have some of these thin skewers on hand when you need a narrow but strong connector, as you do when attaching the heads to the melon swans. The 12-inch skewers are the masts on the sailboats and the tall stems for the vegetable flower arrangements.

Timing

If you're like I am on the day I throw a party, you'll have scant time for creating many garnishes at the last minute. No problem. Almost all garnishes and sculptures can be made up two days ahead. Designs based on sliced pears are the only exception. Pears turn brown within a few hours of being cut. You can retard this a bit by passing your cut pear sections through a bath of undiluted, bottled lemon juice for a few seconds though it will only slow down the browning, not prevent it. The same lemon bath treatment works well on apples. Wedge cuts should be reassembled to minimize their surface area. All garnishes should be wrapped airtight in plastic wrap or bags and refrigerated until needed. Air and heat are the two forces that wilt and dry your garnishes. Wrapped and refrigerated, your creations stay crisp and bright for days. Thus, you needn't wait until the last moment to make them.

Temperature

Low temperatures tend to increase the water pressure in fresh foods, and this pressure tends to make the food split when cut. Happily, most fresh foods can be stored for a half day at room temperature and not suffer. Items you should refrigerate right up to the moment you cut them are: green onions, leeks, Chinese (Napa) cabbage, cauliflower, mushrooms and okra. Carrots and daikon radishes destined to become the trunks of palm trees should also be refrigerated until cut. Once any garnish is created, wrap and refrigerate it.

Soaking & Salting

Vegetable flowers call for a period of soaking in cold water. During this phase the vegetables will absorb some water, swell and expand so as to complete their shaping. It isn't necessary to ice the water, but it should be pre-chilled in your refrigerator. You may also wish to firm up a carrot butterfly with a five minute cold water soak. The times for soaking vary, ranging from five minutes to two days. The specific times are given in the instructions for each garnish on the following pages. Salting food will drain water out of it, rendering the food considerably softer than it is naturally. The carrot fishing net requires soaking the carrot in an extremely salty water bath. Sometimes, a radish fan or other garnish may not want to lay out properly. Then a direct dose of table salt for two or three minutes on the specific area you wish to soften will make the food surprisingly pliable. Be sure to rinse the salt off as soon as the food is soft enough for your needs.

Display Life

All of the designs in this book will last on your buffets for at least four hours. Because the vegetable flowers have so much surface area in relation to their mass, they will begin to wilt a bit during this time but can be kept fresh by water misting via a standard houseplant atomiser. If you want to use them over again, put them back into a cold water bath for a half hour before wrapping and refrigerating. Most of the designs presented on these pages can be used more than once. In general, the larger and more massive an item is, the longer it will stay fresh and reusable.

Transporting

If you need to drive to a party with your creations, pack them into boxes in which you have placed a little towelling to soften their ride.

Keep them wrapped until you arrive. Complete the final assembly of the more fragile designs at the party site. For instance, the wings on the birds should be extended and their heads attached at the party, the fruit skewers should also wait to be added to the watermelon peacock, the arms on the turnip snowman, the wings of the cabbage angel, the sails for the sailboats and the flowers to their stems. In short, if you suspect the rigors of the ride would shake your design apart, you are quite probably correct, and it would prudent to depart a few minutes early and complete your final assembly there.

Summary for Successful Food Sculpturing

1. Work comfortably. Stand on a foot pad, or sit, but work with your back straight. Iluminate your cutting area with a bright light.

2. USE VERY SHARP KNIVES.

3. When slicing, use an exaggerated sawing motion and do not dip or rock your blade. For small, shallow cutting actions, hold your paring knife like a pencil or hold it like a paint brush with the handle in the palm of your hand.

4. DO NOT PUSH OR FORCE YOUR KNIVES.

5. Use two, parallel wooden picks to attach one piece of food to another. Use wooden picks with flat sides.

6. Make your garnishes a day or two ahead; wrap them airtight and store them in the refrigerator. Lemon juice will prevent raw, cut food from browning.

7. Work with fruit and vegetables that have been brought up to room temperature. This prevents splitting or cracking the food. The few exceptions to this rule are noted in the specific design instructions.

8. A cold water bath will swell, expand, open or fix the positions of vegetable flowers. Salting food will soften it.

9. When displaying your garnishes, mist them with cold water to keep them fresh and bright.

10. If you are driving somewhere with your garnishes, wait until you arrive at your destination to complete the final assembly of fragile designs.

11. A little practice goes a long way. My first carrot net was so thick it looked like a carrot horseshoe. Sometimes it took me five tries to get good at a particular cut. There's one real consolation though: in food sculpture you really can eat your mistakes!

Simple Garnishes

These instant garnishing ideas take 5 minutes or less to prepare (though some need a few hours of soaking in cold water to firm them up). Use them to adorn a single plate of food or arrange them on a large platter.

Green Onion Flowers

INGREDIENTS: Green onions with long, unbruised leaves and large firm bottoms.

TOOLS & SUPPLIES: Paring knife, pitcher of cold water.

TIPS & TIMING: Cutting time per flower: about 2 minutes. Soaking time: 20 minutes to 12 hours. It varies from onion to onion so keep an eye on them. Very firm, crisp onions curl up almost instantly. Oversoaking curls them up too tight and gives them a slimy look. After soaking, seal them in a plastic bag, resting them upright among green onion ferns or other vegetable flowers. Laying them flat on their sides will destroy their symmetry.

USES: Arrange 3 or more in a row, along the sides of platters or among crudites and in vegetable flower arrangements.

GREEN ONION DAISY

1. Lay onion on cutting board; slice off 1/4 inch from root end; rings of onion layers should show clearly. If root ends show, cut off another 1/4 inch. Slice off leaves crosswise just below their spreading point. Save leaves for making Green Onion Ferns, page 26.

2. **Insert knife tip to middle of shaft about 2 inches from root end; using a smooth pencil stroke, make a straight cut through root end. Rotate onion slightly; make a second cut, parallel to first and about 1/8 inch from it.** Continue rotating onion and making parallel cuts until you have gone all around shaft. Don't try to take a short cut and make your cuts go all the way through, or you will end up with julienned onion.

3. Gently bend loose strips of onion away from core, opening flower. Soak in cold water until opened.

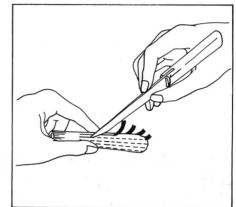

GREEN ONION STAR FLOWER

1. Follow step 1 for Daisy.

2. Hold onion with its root end up. You will need to make about 5 V cuts to form the petals. To make the first cut, rest knife blade along onion's side letting its tip lean in and over top slightly. Use a gentle, downward stroke, pulling knife a bit to the right so the cut goes off at an angle. This cut, which is half of a V, should be 1 inch long.

3. **Complete V by making an opposing cut. The opening at top of V should be 1/4 inch wide. Remove insides of V, and using top of 1 side of your V as a starting point, cut out another V right next to it.** Continue making these narrow V's all around the top. Bend star tips outward and soak in cold water.

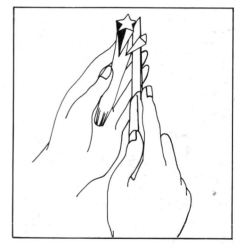

GREEN ONION BRUSH

1. This is a Green Onion Daisy cut at both ends. Leave a good 1/2 inch in center of shaft totally uncut or else design will fall apart. You'll find that the green end will need to be manually bent out in order to match the white end. Soak in cold water. Use as a border, organic chopstick holder or plate accent.

Green Onion Fern

INGREDIENTS: Either a whole green onion, or top of one, whose leaves are securely joined at their bottom. The leaves should be absolutely free of cracks and bruises.

TOOLS & SUPPLIES: Paring knife, deep pitcher of cold water.

TIPS & TIMING: Cutting time: 5 minutes. Soaking time: 10 minutes to 2 hours. Very firm, crisp leaves curl up almost instantly.

USES: Borders for platters, greenery in vegetable flower arrangements. Small sections can be broken off (or make them separately) to use as plate garnishes in lieu of parsley. I am, in spirit, a charter member of "Let's ban parsley as a plate garnish club." Most other fresh herbs are much prettier and far tastier, too.

1. Cut away outer leaves 1 at a time by slipping your knife in between leaf you are removing and onion stalk near base of leaf. Cut away all leaves except 2 leaves nearest new center sprout and center sprout.

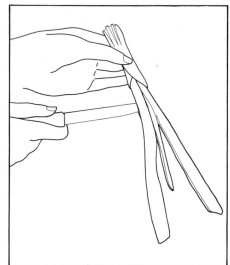

2. Lay onion down. Your onion should have a thin new shoot in its center and 1 leaf on each side of this shoot. These leaves should be 5 to 8 inches long. Generally, these leaves will be rather flat. **Slice each leaf in half lengthwise by inserting your blade through leaf edges at least 1 inch or more from bottom of leaf. If you cut too near bottom, cut leaves curl up into little knots.**

3. Now make same pattern of cuts into each half of each leaf. **Study drawing; notice cuts are straight and begin quite close to 1 side of the leaf. If you start your cuts too far into middle of leaf, the leaf droops. Essentially, you are cutting 3 "blades of grass" up 1 side of leaf and V-cutting top. As you cut, do so down through inside of leaf halves.** This prevents leaves from ripping. Each "blade of grass" should be at least 2 inches long. If your onion is long enough, cut more blades. **Be sure to stagger beginning points of each blade cut. Don't bunch them. One blade begins just below top of blade beneath it.**

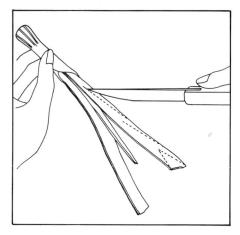

4. After you've made a few of these, you may want to use more than 2 leaves to achieve a fuller fern. Great! Handling more than 4 split sides is a bit awkward though, so proceed carefully.

5. When each half of each leaf has been given a pattern of "blade" cuts, carefully immerse onion in a water bath, being sure not to bend or break any of fragile leaves. The blades will quickly begin to curl up. Remove "Fern", seal it in a plastic bag and refrigerate, once it has curled to your liking.

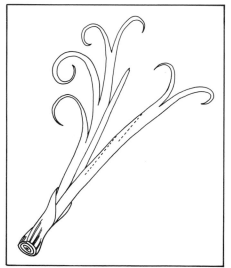

Flowers from Chilies & Fresh Peppers

INGREDIENTS: Chili flowers: Bright yellow, orange or red chilies, 2 to 3 inches long and tapering to a sharp point. Pepper flowers: Small conical yellow or red bell peppers.

TOOLS & SUPPLIES: Paring knife, rubber gloves (This design is HOT! It looks hot and feels hot! Wear those rubber gloves when you hold chilies.) and a pitcher of cold water for soaking chilies.

TIPS & TIMING: Cutting time per chili flower: 2 to 3 minutes. Pepper flower: 5 minutes. Soaking times: 8 hours to 2 days. Chilies and peppers that are red and have thin skin open faster. Flowers will continue to open a bit after they are removed from the water so don't over-soak them. These flowers are hardy and can be re-used 2 or 3 times.

USES: Because pepper flowers are large they may overwhelm a vegetable-flowers-in-a-vase arrangement. However, a small star cut from flower end of pepper works well in a standard arrangement, and you can attach a green onion daisy to its center for a lively effect. Generally, pepper flowers are displayed in the center of an hors d'oeuvre platter. The chili flowers can be used on platters and in vase arrangements, adding thematic support to Mexican and Oriental buffets, in particular.

CHILI FLOWER

1. Lay chili on cutting board; slice off stem but don't cut into actual chili. Insert tip of paring knife through skin about 1/2 inch in from stem end; don't cut into seed pod.

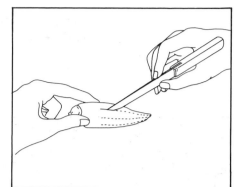

2. **Now draw knife in a straight line out through tip of chili. Rotate chili slightly (less than a quarter-turn); repeat this cut.** Continue making cuts at same distance from each other—a bit less than a quarter turn apart, making a total of 5 cuts, and consequently, 5 petals in your flower.

3. Insert your blade through 1 petal cut; carefully saw your way around inside of all petals cutting through ribs of pithy tissue that connect skin to seed pod.

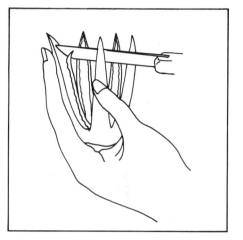

4. **One at a time, bend petals out and shave inside of each petal smooth.** Insert tip of knife blade into base of chili and cut all around bottom of seed pod, making sure skin is well separated from seeds. Leave seed pod in place. Soak chili until it curls open.

PEPPER FLOWER

1. Trim stem off a firm, small red or yellow bell pepper. Lay pepper on its stem end. Cut out a 5-pointed star from the blossom end. The points should be 1-1/2 inches long with the center body a little bigger than length of 1 point. Twist off star. It doesn't need soaking; just use it as a colorful addition to your flower arrangement.

2. Treat the remaining large part of pepper just like a chili flower. Cutting off the star left V-shaped openings down the sides of this larger piece. **Cut down from bottom of these V's to stem end of pepper to create petals.** Cut notches out from sides of petals, if you like. Cut off all connective tissue between skin and seeds. Soak for at least 1 day. When displaying these, you may attach Green Onion Daisies, page 25, into tip of each seed pod with wooden picks.

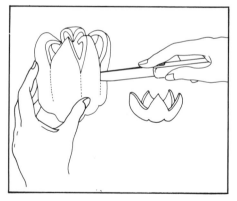

Carrot Spider Mum

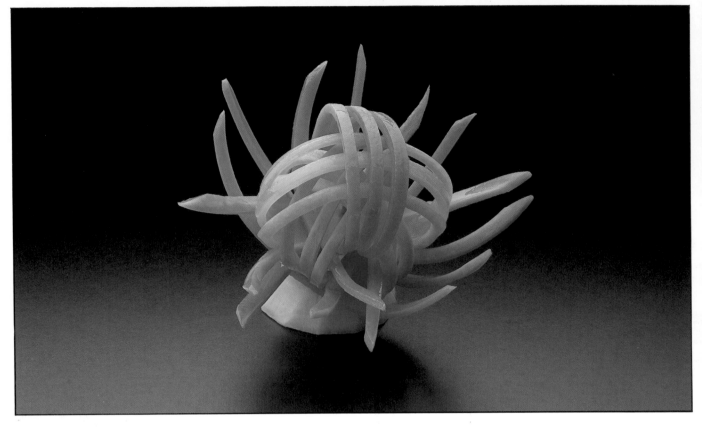

INGREDIENTS: A large, straight, room-temperature carrot 7 inches long and 1 inch wide for all 7 inches.

TOOLS & SUPPLIES: A 9-inch chef's knife, paring knife, bamboo skewer and a glass of cold water.

TIPS & TIMING: Cutting time: 5 to 10 minutes. Assembly: 2 minutes. Soaking: 30 minutes. Carrots that are cold have a tendency to crack so let them warm up well before cutting.

USES: A lively flower for your "Vegetable Flowers-in-a-Vase" arrangement. By substituting a strong wooden pick for skewer or simply cutting off skewer just below completed flower, you can use this design as a platter or cutting board garnish.

1. Don't peel carrot; cut to make a straight, 7-inch length. Conserving as much of carrot's width as possible, slice off 3 sides, making right angle cuts.

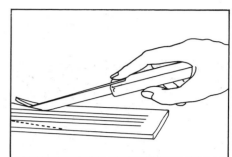

2. Using uncut side as "back", saw-cut 4 or more slices that are as thick as a nickel off "front" side. Slices should be even in thickness all along their length.

3. **Lengthwise cut 4 slits, equal distance apart, through each slice, leaving 1 inch uncut at each end. This yields slices with 5 bands.**

4. **Diagonally cut 2 outer bands of each slice in half, making their ends pointed.**

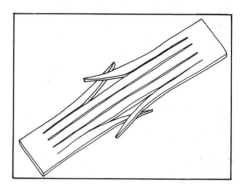

5. **Bend 1 strip into a loop, overlapping its uncut ends. Gently push (with a slight twisting motion) point of a bamboo skewer through center of overlapped ends, until point is through both layers and sticking into loop 1/2 inch.**

6. Insert 1 end of a second strip into this loop and press it onto skewer. It's best to angle this second strip so it crisscrosses direction of first strip. Fold this strip up, over and back into loop, pressing its other end down onto tip of skewer. Keep feeding skewer into loop so its tip remains exposed. Now continue adding 1 or 2 more strips in same fashion at various angles, forming a ball-like shape out of bands.

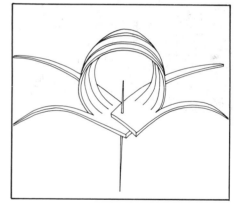

7. Cup finished flower in your hand folding loose bands up around ball. Set it in this position into a glass of cold water to fix spikes into upright position. Be sure whole flower is immersed. Soak it for 1/2 hour. Check flower. If spikes still spring out too much for your taste, soak it a little longer. Tightly wrap finished flower in plastic and refrigerate. Display this flower as is or daub its top with a little honey and sprinkle poppy seeds onto honey. This will give flower a tiger lily coloration.

Red Radish Rosette

INGREDIENTS: Firm, room-temperature, large, tulip-shaped, red radishes.

TOOLS AND SUPPLIES: Paring knife, cold water bath.

TIPS & TIMING: Use large, tulip-shaped or at least long radishes. Cutting time: about 5 minutes. Soaking time: 8 hours, or more. Make a few extras; not all radishes open equally well. Around my house I have to makes lots of extras—my wife eats them like popcorn!

USES: Vegetable flower arrangements, as a crudité and a plate garnish.

1. Slice off stem so radish rests on your board with its root standing straight up.

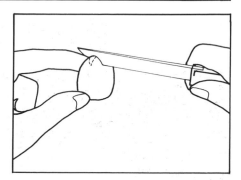

2. **Using a gentle saw-cut, make a wedge from center of top, slicing 1 side of a V about 1/4-inch deep, then making an opposing cut, removing root in process.** If your radish has a very long, tapering shape, cut a 1/2-inch deep V.

3. Cut 2 more V's into top of radish; position these V's like an X over first V. This placement of V-cut wedges yields 6 red, pointed peaks.

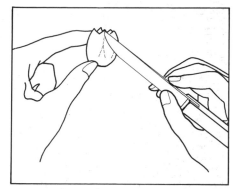

4. You now cut "petals" under each peak. **For a petal, insert your knife point about 1/8 inch directly beneath a red peak, and aiming in from 1 side of peak, just slice down side of radish, keeping knife point directly under red peak. The angle of blade is shallow. Don't aim your knife into center of radish. This would make a petal too thick to open up. As you near bottom withdraw your blade. This single cut makes 1/2 of 1 petal.** Turn radish and re-insert tip of your knife so it intersects top of first cut. Draw blade straight down cutting opposite side of petal. The petal should be a bit loose to touch. If petal doesn't wiggle, then whittle it at its bottom to weaken it. Manually, bend each petal outward.

5. Repeat this petal-making step under each red peak. Leave a border of red skin around each petal. Soak in cold water for at least 8 hours, allowing petals to swell out from body of radish.

Radish Jacks, Mushrooms & Fans

INGREDIENTS: Red radishes at room temperature. Table salt for fan.

TOOLS & SUPPLIES: A paring knife.

TIPS & TIMING: The "Jacks" should be made up just before using them. The "mushrooms" and fans can be made a day ahead. The Jacks take 30 seconds to cut and assemble. The mushrooms take 1 minute each. The fans take 2 minutes to cut and 20 minutes to soften after salting.

USES: The Jacks are salad garnishes, crudités and platter border material. The mushrooms garnish salads and are also crudités. When secured to a base with wooden picks, mushrooms can be used on cutting boards and as platter centerpiece items. The fans are very salty and should therefore be used only as accents on cutting boards.

JACKS

1. Use a radish with a round or cylindrical shape. **Cut it crosswise into slices slightly thinner than a nickel. Insert tip of your knife into center of a slice; cut a straight line to side.** (First 2 illustrations.) Use 2 cut slices for 1 Jack.

2. In each hand, pick up 1 cut slice. Hold 1 vertically, the other, horizontally with open cuts in each slice facing each other. Bend 1 coin to open its cut and slide the 2 coins onto each other. If you do this with coins at right angles to each other, they will lock in place.

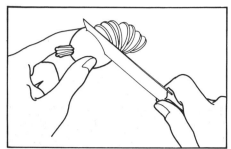

MUSHROOMS

1. Cut off root and stem, conserving as much of body of radish as possible. **Hold radish in 1 hand, root up. Position blade so it is flat and facing into radish at a point about 1/3 of way down its side. Cut halfway into center of radish.** (Don't cut half way through it. Halfway to center means you cut only 1/4 of way through radish.) With your knife held at this depth, rotate radish 1 full turn.

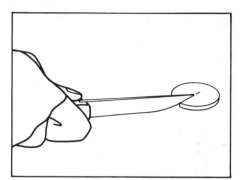

2. **Remove blade and reposition it so it is aiming up into stem end of radish about same depth in from side as depth of your rotating cut. Now cut up to rotating cut. This will remove a piece of outside of radish from bottom 2/3 of its body and leaves some of its center intact. Continue this, paring away outside of bottom of whole radish and leaving center intact.** The center is mushroom stem. The mushroom cap is uncut 1/3 left at root end. Slice little circles of skin off cap for a brighter looking mushroom.

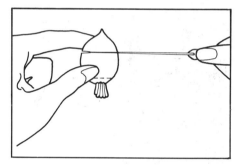

FAN

1. Use a very evenly shaped, rather large radish. Keep any fresh, unbruised leaves on radish. Cut away root.

2. Hold radish down on your cutting board. The key to making fan is holding your blade straight up and down as you make perfectly parallel cuts. The cuts run from stem end to root. They are open at root end. Begin on right side if you're right handed. If left handed, you start from left side. Carefully, hold your blade so tip is about 1/8 inch away from top edge of radish. Since radish is somewhat round, the tip of blade will be nearer stem when you get to middle. Therefore, beginning of cuts follows an arc.

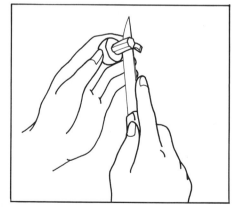

3. Once you have cut parallel slices all across radish, hold it up and sprinkle salt down into each cut, but do not salt leaves.

Rolled Vegetable Flowers

INGREDIENTS: Large, room temperature rutabaga, turnip or beet, 3 to 4 inches wide.

TOOLS & SUPPLIES: These flowers are made with very thin vegetable slices. Wash and trim ends from rutabaga, turnip and beet. Take these to a delicatessen or butcher and have them sliced into rounds thin enough to fold over without cracking—almost as thin as a postcard. You'll pay a token fee to have this done, but it's just impossible to cut them by hand. A large turnip yields about 40 slices. Use 4 or 5 slices for 1 flower. You'll also need wooden picks and a cold water bath.

TIPS & TIMING: Each flower, once slicing is done, takes just a couple of minutes to fold. Don't delay folding them once slices have been made. Even when wrapped, slices soon become fragile. After folding flowers, give them 5 minutes in cold water to firm up. Then seal in plastic and refrigerate until needed. They won't turn brown.

USES: In vegetable flower arrangements or as platter center pieces. (You can also do this with potatoes; deep-fry them and serve.)

1. You may make these flowers using just 1 vegetable or you can mix 2 or 3 in same flower. Roll first slice into a tight cylinder. The center of cylinder must be solid. The slice may crack at first. Just keep rolling, cracking will stop. Now roll a second slice around first. Don't line them up evenly. Let first cylinder stick out from second 1/2 inch. (You can substitute a thin carrot stick for first cylinder, if you wish.)

2. **Holding rolled cylinder in 1 hand, wrap bottom half of another slice around it, letting top half of this new slice fall away from core. Overlap 2 sides of bottom of this new slice and manually hold it all together.**

3. **Add another slice to arrangement just under and/or opposite of preceding slice, letting more of this new slice fall away from central core.** Now flower becomes difficult to handle. You can stop here or go on adding more slices. If you add more, lay next slice on from opposite side. (The potato flower looks best with 6 or 7 petals.)

4. Secure flowers with 2 or 3 wooden picks set through bottoms of "petal" slices, passing through core and out other side. Crisscross picks without piercing the petals' edges. Set flower to soak in cold water. The petals will firm up in a few minutes. Place flowers in a plastic bag and refrigerate. Don't be concerned about wooden picks; they are snipped off with scissors before displaying flowers.

SALAMI FLOWER

You can make a flower out of salami slices too! Use hard salami and proceed as per rolled flower instructions. It's possible to use up to 10 slices of salami to create a striking accent to an antipasto platter.

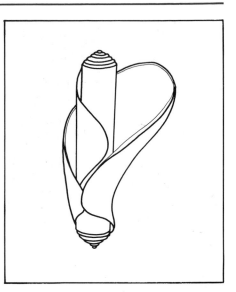

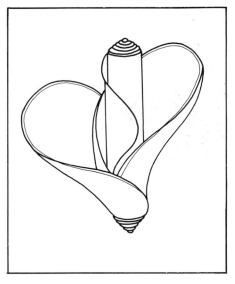

Vegetable Vase & Flower Arrangement

INGREDIENTS: Any heavy, solid fruit or vegetable for vase—a butternut squash is best, but a head of cauliflower or unripe melon will suffice. Green onion leaves to cover skewers and assorted vegetable flowers.

TOOLS & SUPPLIES: 12 (8- to 12-inch) bamboo skewers, chef's knife, paring knife, scoring tool, zester and a small, sharp melon baller.

TIPS & TIMING: The butternut squash works best because it already looks like a flower vase, has a low center of gravity, and therefore won't easily topple over. It carves cleanly, doesn't discolor, is firm and will hold skewers in place. You can carve vase 3 or 4 days in advance.

USE: As a free-standing table top decoration.

1. With a large knife, slice 1/2-inch off bottom of squash so it will rest flat. Be sure angle of cut allows neck of squash to stand straight up.

2. **Slice off top of neck.** Leave this cut alone or cut out V shapes from around its sides, use a melon baller to scoop round cavities or carve steps into your V's.

3. Use your scorer, zester, paring knife and melon baller to carve as simple or complex a pattern as you like into surface of squash.

4. **Insert a dozen skewers into top of neck. If they are hard to push in, poke holes into squash with an ice pick, then push skewers into those holes. Keep angles of skewers fairly vertical but try to fan them out somewhat, some high, some low.**

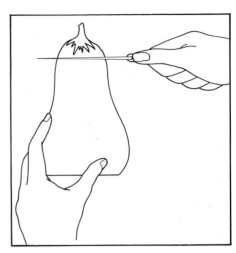

5. Now cover skewers by slipping green onion leaves over them. Wrap vase and skewers as a unit, in plastic, and store in refrigerator a few days. Just before you are going to display your arrangement, unwrap skewered vase and stick flowers and ferns onto tops of skewers. However, if you have made Carrot Spider Mums, remember that they are already on skewers, so be sure to leave room for them if you are placing skewers in the vase in advance. If you do skewering just prior to displaying your arrangement, begin with Mums, remembering to slip green onion leaves over their skewers before sticking them into vase.

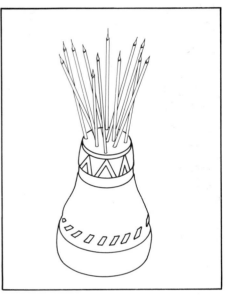

6. Occasionally mist flowers with a fine spray of water while they are on display. Don't announce that the flowers are made from vegetables. Your guests will eventually notice your flowers' novelty and enjoy their own sense of surprised discovery all the more.

N-Cut Twists

INGREDIENTS: These can be made from carrots, Daikon radishes, turnips, citrus peels, slices of cucumber or virtually any firm yet flexible fresh fruit or vegetable.

TOOLS & SUPPLIES: Paring knife or 6-inch knife.

TIPS & TIMING: One of the easiest and quickest garnishes to make, these twists can be cut at the last minute or made up a few hours in advance if wrapped airtight and refrigerated.

USES: Crudités, individual plate garnishes, accents in salads, borders for bowls and platters.

1. For solid foods (carrots, turnips, etc.) cut a rectangular block 3 times longer than its width. For cucumbers and citrus peels, you must prepare each twist individually by cutting a slice about 2 inches long, 3/4 inch wide and slightly less than 1/4 inch thick.

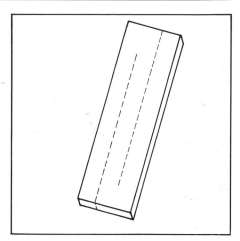

2. Cut solid block into slices thick enough to bend into a "C" shape without breaking. If your block is tiny—an inch long, for instance, slices should be as thin as a dime. If block is 3 inches long, then make slices as thick as 2 nickels.

3. **To make twist, cut each slice twice. The first cut is made 1/3 of way in from right side beginning at a point 1/5 of way down from top.** This cut goes down along length of slice, parallel to its right side, and continues all way out through bottom. **Spin slice around so top is now at bottom and right side now on left. Repeat cut.**

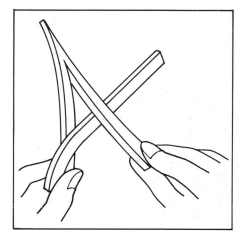

4. The slice is now cut like a letter N. Each of its 3 "legs" is of equal width.

5. Complete the design by twisting the 2 side legs over the center, bending 1 behind the other.

Tomato Rose

INGREDIENTS: A round, firm tomato.

TOOLS & SUPPLIES: A 6-inch knife.

TIPS & TIMING: Use a gentle sawing motion. Peeling a tomato can be quite messy if you push too hard with your knife. Roses can be made with cherry tomatoes and citrus fruits, but start with regular tomatoes first. Citrus-peel roses must be cut paper thin.

The roses can be made up a day in advance. It's convenient to lay them on cucumber slices and then handle them by lifting slices rather than roses.

USES: Place a single rose, or a bouquet of 3 or more, on any flat serving dish, tray or board as a centerpiece or corner accent. Surround roses with fresh green herbs. Place 1 in center of a cucumber spiral for a double design— very striking! Cherry tomato roses are lovely garnishes for individual plates. Do not place tomato roses on top of bowls of salad for they will unravel as salad is being served and your tomato rose will become a tomato snake.

1. **Begin by cutting a 1/2-inch wide strip of skin from around stem depression, using a gentle sawing motion. Leave a little flesh attached to skin but stay well out of seed area.** The knife doesn't advance very much. Rather, tomato should be rotated into sawing blade. Don't rush, but do keep a light and steady pressure behind your sawing motion.

2. Just as you are about to complete cutting this strip from around stem depression, dip angle of knife so second turn around tomato will be just under first. The rest of the process is to peel a continuous strip of skin from entire tomato. Generally, 3 to 4 full revolutions can be made before finishing. As ribbon of skin lengthens, work so it can rest on your cutting board. If ribbon breaks somewhere near its middle, don't fret. Overlapping pieces during final roll-up will correct that problem.

3. As you near very end of cutting, finish by slicing a slightly wider swatch of skin through last inch or so.

4. **Lay ribbon out flat, skin side down. It will form an elongated "S." Begin rolling it up in reverse; that is, begin at flower end.** It's easiest to leave it on cutting board rather than holding it up in your hands. Pretend you're rolling up some leftover ribbon. As you near stem end, follow curving peel all way around. No special twisting should occur. You are now finished. If your rose looks odd, you have probably done what at least half of all cooks do— you've managed to turn it upside down while rolling peel onto stem end. Just turn it over.

5. If you'd like a rose that looks more like a rosebud, lay peel skin side up before rolling it.

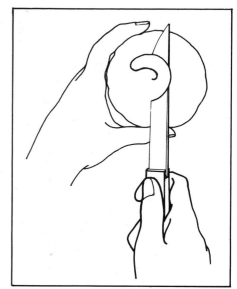

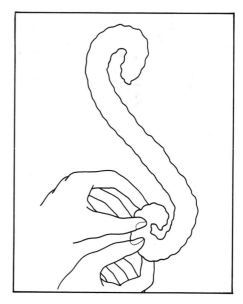

Turned Mushroom

INGREDIENTS: Fresh mushrooms with smooth, dome-shaped caps and a little lemon juice to keep them white.

TOOLS & SUPPLIES: A paring knife.

TIPS & TIMING: Although this garnish is quite simple in its design and technique, it is not easy to do. The common pitfall is a tendency to slice forward rather than using a cutting stroke that slides blade **down** its length. It simply takes a bit of practice but once you've learned to do it correctly, a turned mushroom can be cut in less than a minute. If you are using them as cold food garnishes, pass finished mushrooms through a dilute lemon-water mixture for a few seconds to prevent them from browning.

USES: Served cold, turned mushrooms are appropriate on salads, luncheon plates, meat trays and on crudites platters. They are, however, perfect garnishes for steaks and hot roasts and can be served warm by **briefly** sautéing them in butter just before serving.

1. Slice stem so it is flush with bottom of cap. Peel cap by scraping strips of its skin up and away from around bottom. As each strip comes loose, pinch it between your thumb and blade and pull strip away, up to top of cap where it will break off.

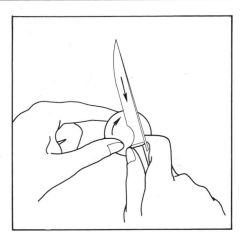

2. The turned mushroom is made by cutting out shallow grooves that radiate from center of top down around sides as described in step 3. These grooves should widen a bit as they approach bottom of cap. This is accomplished by flattening the angle of knife blade as you approach bottom of each groove. The grooves should border each other. If you are right-handed, make each successive cut immediately to right of preceding groove; to left, if you are left-handed. Otherwise knife will be covering preceding cut and you won't be able to position your blade so next groove is bordering groove before it.

3. **The actual cut is made by laying the heel of blade onto center of top of cap at a 45 degree angle. You may hold your knife with its tip pointing away from you or pointing toward you whichever way feels more natural to you. Now cut into cap about 1/16 inch deep. Begin to slide blade toward its handle (away from center of cap).** This is a critical point: rock tip of blade forward (in direction of its cutting edge just slightly) as you slide knife down away from cap's top. A small strip of mushroom will begin to peel up over your blade.

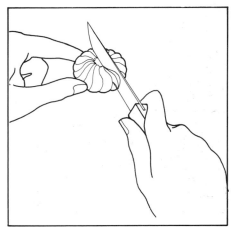

4. Finish cut by continuing to slide your blade along its length going down side of cap and, as you do so, roll cap up along knife. At beginning of cut, knife is doing most of moving. As you proceed with cut, cap takes over most of movement. Note that cap and blade are travelling in opposite directions. The small strip of mushroom will widen and peel away as you cut.

5. **Repeat this groove-making cut again and again until entire surface of cap has been reshaped with shallow, adjacent, radiant grooves. The natural turning motion of your wrist made by rolling (turning) cap over will automatically produce swirls.**

6. The mushroom is now "turned" and can be left as is. An optional finishing touch may be achieved by slicing off very top of cap leaving a flat surface there. This surface may be drawn on with point of your knife. You can etch in a flower, sunburst, a flying bird or a star. To make a star, simply lay tip of your blade onto flat surface and rock its point down into cap. Lift blade, rotate cap and repeat rocking-pressing action with tip of your blade until you've made 5 points.

Cucumber Fans

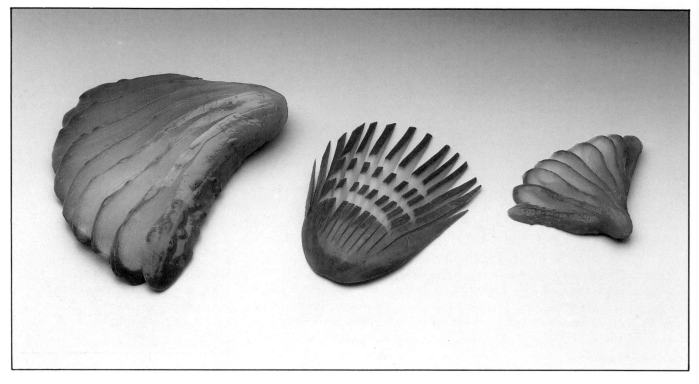

INGREDIENTS: A firm cucumber or small cucumber pickle (gherkins or cornichons).

TOOLS & SUPPLIES: A paring knife for pickles; a 6-inch knife for cucumbers.

TIPS & TIMING: The pickled gherkins and cornichons can be cut while still cold. Cucumbers must be room temperature to prevent them from cracking. Fans can be made a day in advance. Simply make cuts, wrap and refrigerate until needed. Spread them into their open position at time of display. Cutting time: 5 minutes.

USES: Fresh cucumber fans are suitable accents on carving boards and platters. Cornichon and gherkin fans are for cold meat trays and individual plates on which cold meats are served.

1. To fan gherkins and cornichons, place on a cutting board; trim off stems. Insert point of paring knife 1/5 of the way from stem end and just inside 1 side of pickle. Pass point of blade all way down to cutting board and draw it down length of pickle making a slice all along that side. The slice should be thin enough to be easily bent. For tiny cornichons this will be as thin as a dime, for gherkins, the thickness of a nickel. Proceed to cut slices parallel to first 1 until you have done so all across width of pickle. To fan them out, press down onto beginning point of cuts near stem and with your thumb and, as you press down, push a little to either side of pickle. It will fan out. If it doesn't, check your cuts. They need to have gone completely down through pickle in order to achieve flexibility required to create a fan.

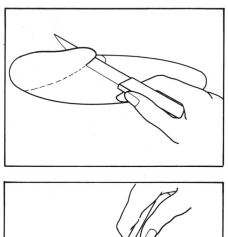

2. **To make cucumber fans, begin by inserting cutting edge of your 6-inch knife 3 to 4 inches from 1 end. Holding your blade at a shallow (20 degrees) angle, cut off a wedge that is no more than 1/2 inch thick at final end.** This wedge **is cut into a fan as for the pickles by inserting your blade at thick end so open end of fan appears at thin end of cucumber wedge. Slices should be just slightly thicker than a nickel.** Up to 4 fans can be made from 1 cucumber.

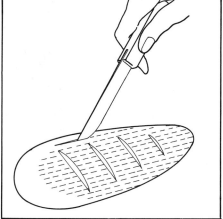

3. A more attractive fan can be made by cutting wedges in skin side of cucumber wedge before making your parallel slices. Keep wedges quite narrow and shallow. Also, be sure to line them up across *width* of wedge.

4. If your fan doesn't open easily by pressing down on its thicker, joined end, shave a bit of cucumber flesh off underside of joined end.

Upright Cucumber Fans

INGREDIENTS: A firm, room temperature cucumber.

TOOLS & SUPPLIES: A 6-inch knife.

TIPS & TIMING: A hothouse (sometimes called an English) cucumber is less seedy than a regular cucumber and will make a stronger upright fan. You can make this a day or so in advance. Wrap and refrigerate, unspread.

USES: Fans with 3 slices are suitable as individual plate garnishes and as borders on boards or platters. Fans having 5, 7 or 9 slices can be used to accent centers or ends of platters and corners of cutting boards.

1. Slice cucumber in half lengthwise.

2. Lay 1 half flat-side-down on cutting board. **Position knife so it is aimed across width of cucumber on a diagonal so that slice will be 3 inches long. Make cut, removing end of cucumber.**

3. **Now you are going to make an odd number of slices (3, 5, 7) parallel to cut made in step 2 without cutting slices loose. To make slices, hold blade so its point is about 1/2 inch in from far side of cucumber and blade is parallel to side you created with cut in step 2 and in from that side about the thickness of a nickel. Gently saw cut your way straight down to cutting board. Repeat this cut again and again until you have odd number you want. The final cut is made completely across cucumber, thus freeing fan from main body of cucumber.**

4. Leave slices on both ends of your fan as is. One by one, bend second slice (also fourth, sixth and eighth slices, if you've made these) around into a loop so its end is tucked back alongside its own beginning point. Go about this bending maneuver very carefully. If your slices are too thick they will break. One solution is to sprinkle a little salt over slices to soften them. It's hard to stop this softening process, however, and you may end up with a fan too soft to stand upright. A better solution is to start over, cutting longer, thinner slices.

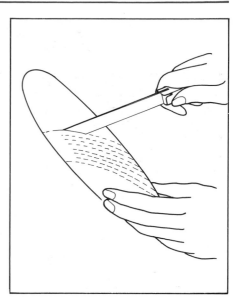

Cucumber Spiral

INGREDIENTS: A firm, unbruised, room temperature cucumber.

TOOLS & SUPPLIES: A 6-inch knife, an 8-inch wooden dowel 1/4 inch thick and a wooden pick.

TIPS & TIMING: This design also works very well with a hothouse cucumber or a large but tender zucchini. Dowels can be purchased at most lumber or hardware stores. Make spiral up to 2 days ahead. Store it in its original cucumber shape, wrapped and refrigerated. Extend it into a spiral just before displaying it.

USES: A perfect centerpiece for round platters. Display it alone or rest a tomato rose in its center.

1. Slice both ends off cucumber leaving a center section about 6 inches long.

2. Pass wooden dowel lengthwise through center of cucumber.

3. **Hold dowelled cucumber horizontally in front of your chest. You are going to be turning or, rather, rolling cucumber over and over. It will break if you try to do this on cutting board.**

4. **Holding cucumber in 1 hand, lay your knife so center of blade is resting on surface of cucumber at its right end (if you're right-handed, left side for left-handed cooks). Aim your blade straight down toward dowel but also tilt it so that its tip is headed in toward body of cucumber slightly, about 10 degrees. Gently press blade into cucumber and onto dowel.**

5. Holding blade against dowel, begin rotating cucumber so its top is rolling toward you. As you rotate cucumber, your blade will go into body of cucumber. After 1 full revolution knife should be about 1/4 inch from original point of insertion.

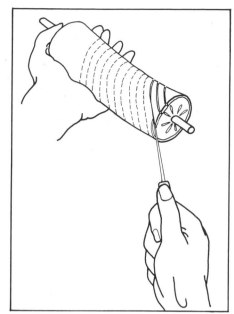

6. Continue rotating cucumber over and over, always maintaining a constant 1/4 inch from preceding cut.

7. After about 10 full turns, you will have enough to create a spiral. You need not cut all the way down length of cucumber. Finish spiral by gradually shifting angle of your blade into preceding turn. This completes cutting. Slip spiral off dowel.

8. Bend ends of cucumber around so they fit up against each other forming a circular spiral. Break a 1/2-inch piece off a wooden pick; insert piece through 2 joined ends of cucumber at inside of circle.

9. After you have done this a few times you may feel confident about making a more delicate spiral—one whose pathway is closer together. These thin-walled spirals can be laid out straight along sides of platters to form borders.

Red Radish Mice

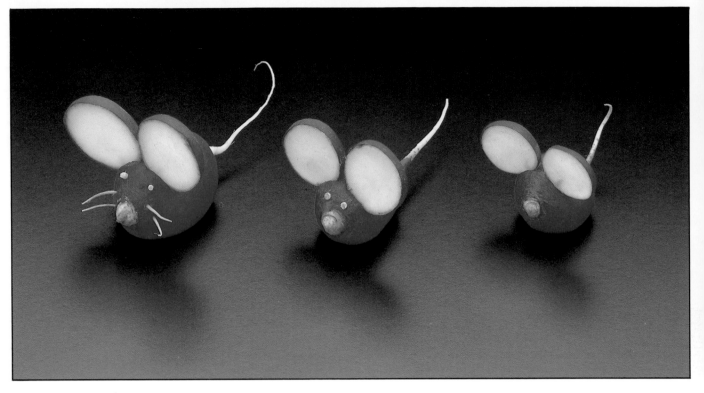

INGREDIENTS: One bunch of red radishes with their stems and roots intact.

TOOLS & SUPPLIES: A paring knife and a wooden pick.

TIPS & TIMING: Each mouse takes 2 minutes to cut. If made a day ahead, secure ears with wooden picks as described in step 5.

USES: Perfect for cheese boards. Make a family of mice, mama, papa and baby. These are also fun at Christmas parties—when not a creature was stirring, not even a red radish mouse.

1. The radish root will be the tail of the mouse, so be sure to leave it on. Usually these roots are curved. Your first cut is a thin slice off 1 side of radish. The side to cut is the 1 opposite the direction of natural curve of root. Now lay radish on this cut side. Its root should be curving up.

2. To make nose, first cut off stems about 1/4 inch from radish. Pare remaining stub of stems into a small nose cone.

3. **The ears are 2 oversized, round slices cut from another radish. Slices about sizes of pennies or nickels work quite well.**

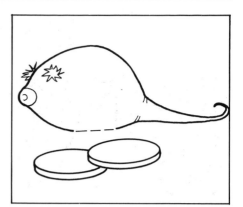

4. Each ear is attached by fitting snugly into a slit cut into each side of radish just back from nose. These slits are near top of radish in line with each other but they do not meet at top. Keep them apart by 1/8 inch or more. If they are too close, ears will bump each other out of their respective slits. **To make each slit, hold your knife in a pencil grip and make 2 short, parallel cuts straight down about 1/4 inch deep. Space your cuts so ears slices will fit very tightly into slits.** With your knife point pop out section of radish from between these 2 cuts.

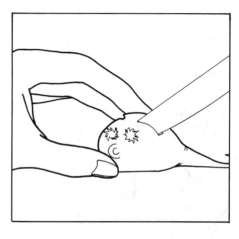

5. If ears fall out of slits, cut thicker ears. To make sure ears will stay in place for a long time you need to attach them by means of thin wooden picks. Cut off 1/2 inch of each end of a wooden pick. Make these cuts on an extreme diagonal so each little end piece is pointed on both of its ends. Slip finer point into edge of each ear slice, then push ear slice down into slit, pick first.

6. You can add eyes by sticking tiny cloves or small bits of wooden pick into radish just in front of ears.

7. Whiskers can be made with extra radish or green onion roots. Use a wooden pick to poke 3 holes on each side of radish just back from nose. Insert a single length of root into each hole. The length of whiskers is up to you. Long whiskers create a very comical effect.

Wedge Cuts:
THE MAKING OF WINGS

Wings for the apple duck, apple swan, pear quail, kiwifruit songbird, squash geese, melon duck and melon swan are all cut the same way. In addition, individual plate garnishes of simple wing sets can be made from practically any round or even partially round food: olives, radishes, zucchini, plums, peaches, and even strawberries.

The key to successfully making these wing sets is to use a blade that is longer than the food you are cutting across. There is no delicate modelling or fancy sculpting going on in cutting of wings. It is all straight slicing. The wedges (wing sections) will automatically come out with rounded tops, straight sides and pointed ends. Another key to success is controlling the depth of your cuts; use the *saw cut* that is described on page 21.

Study the drawing for a moment. Notice how there are two distinct wedge shapes. One is a V. The other is a bit more open and tends to be L shaped. The V wedge is used to make the wings out of the top of a food. The L-shaped wedges are used on the sides of food. In both cases, the wing sets are simply a series of wedges. See how the bottoms of the wedges in each series are all lined up straight. You always begin by cutting the smallest wedge first. Then you make the second to the smallest wedge and so on.

The biggest pitfall in cutting wedges is pushing your knife too far. When this happens, the sides of the next wedge you cut in that set will come out separately rather than in the normal joined position. However, even if this happens once or twice in a set, you can still succeed. Just keep your individual pieces together and when you are putting your bird wings back into the body, go ahead and use the separated sides in their proper position as if they weren't disconnected. Gravity and the tendency for moist food to stick to itself will hold your broken wing sections in place. Now, if every wing in the set happens to come away in two pieces, well, you've just made a rather arduous start on a wonderful salad, but you won't have come very far as a bird carver. Start

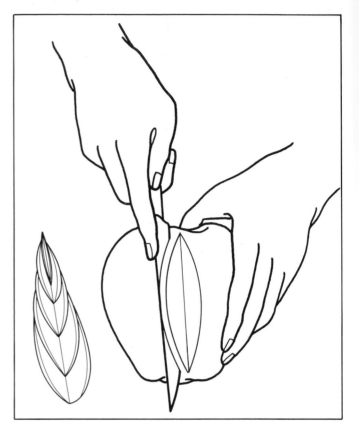

over and DON'T PUSH ON THE KNIFE. USE A GENTLE SAWING MOTION.

THE V CUT

1. In most cases, you'll be cutting wings out of a piece of food from which you've already cut a slice to make the bird's head. Rest the food on the flat side from which the slice was taken, whenever possible. Whatever you're cutting, hold it firmly on the board.

2. Hold your blade level and over the center of the top of the food, going from front to back. Move the blade 1/8 inch to the right and angle it in toward the center. The slope of this angle should be just like the slope of the right half of the letter V. Saw cut your way into the food. Stop when the cutting edge of your knife is right under the center of the food. Withdraw the blade.

3. Now make the opposite cut in from the left. It is a mirror image of the first and completes the letter V. Lift the resulting wedge out on the side of your blade and set it on your board.

4. All successive wedges in this wing set are cut the same way. Just begin each cut a little to the outside of the V-shaped cavity and finish each cut directly under the bottom of the V-shaped cavity.

5. If you find it hard to make the cut from the left but can do it well from the right side (or vice-versa), it's perfectly all right to give the food a half turn between each cut so you will always be cutting in from the right.

THE L CUT

1. The L-shaped wedges differ only in the angle of the slopes. Otherwise, follow the saw cutting technique for the V-shaped wedges. Cut the more vertical stroke first. Then make the second cut aiming for the bottom of the vertical stroke.

2. Be sure the second cut (the more horizontal one) does angle down into the food slightly. If you cut up into the food, the side wings will tend to slip down and out of their cavity. The exact distances between cuts and the recommended angles for the wedges vary a little from bird to bird. These measurements are given in the instructions for each bird.

PATTERNS

When you make apple birds and melon birds use the traceable drawings on page 139-141 to carve the heads. Simply copy the design you need onto ordinary tracing paper. Then cut out your traced design with a pair of scissors and use the pattern as outlined in the instructions. If the apple or melon that you use is unusually small or large, you may need to make the heads slightly smaller or larger than the pattern to keep the correct proportion. If you intend to carve some or all of the birds rather often, you should tape your paper pattern onto a sheet of colored plastic called acetate and then cut pattern out of acetate. The acetate is available at art supply stores. These plastic patterns will last through dozens of uses. Simply wipe them dry after each use and store them flat in your book.

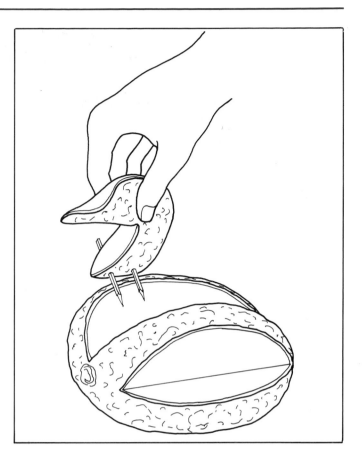

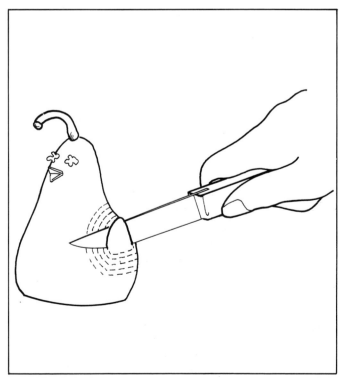

Apple Duck & Apple Swan

INGREDIENTS: For each bird: 1 large Red Delicious apple, 1/4 cup lemon juice in a saucer.

TOOLS & SUPPLIES: Paring knife, 6-inch knife, 1 wooden pick and apple duck and swan patterns on pages 139-141.

TIPS & TIMING: Duck takes 10 minutes; swan a few minutes more. Birds can be made 2 days ahead. The lemon juice keeps them from browning. Dip every wedge and head in juice as soon as they are completed. For storing, leave wings unextended. Wrap birds tightly and refrigerate. If you display 2 ducks (or swans) with their beaks touching, carve 1 head with beak facing right and other facing left.

USES: Centerpieces for platters and cheese boards. Free-standing table decorations.

DUCK

1. Remove stem. Set apple on stem end. Take a slice off 1 side, starting with blade going down through 2 of the little bumps and cutting straight down. Place your apple duck pattern on flat side of this slice with beak pointing toward end with bumps. If you're righthanded, have beak pointing to right. Lightly trace outline into apple. Remove and wipe pattern dry. Block-cut around traced design. It is important to hold your knife at a right angle as you cut. Begin saw cutting at front of beak. Saw cut with your paring knife using short, gentle strokes. Cut along top of beak going up over head and down back of neck in 1 continuous move. See second illustration on page 59 for example. Now, cut front of neck and bottom of beak. Shave square edge off top of beak on fleshy side. You can also trim a bit of skin from top of beak; but do not cut any of forehead away. Set aside.

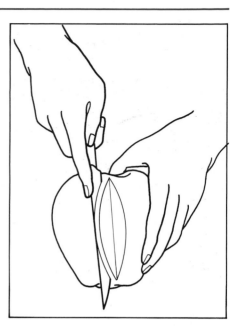

2. There are 3 sets of wings. Imagine the apple's stem end is a clock face. Begin the first set at the top—12 o'clock. The wedge runs lengthwise from end to end. **The first wedge is a little over 1 inch long and up to 1/4 inch wide at its middle. The walls of each successive wedge are as thick as a nickel.** Make 5 V-shaped wedges, or more. Stop before your reach middle of apple.

3. The L-shaped side wing sets begin at 2:30 and 9:30. If you're right-handed, begin at 2:30 (right side). After cutting the right set, turn apple around so left side is now on your right; make final set. It's much easier to always cut side wings in from the side you naturally hold your knife.

4. To attach the duck head, trim fleshy side of bottom of neck so it fits snugly in stem end of top V-shaped cavity. Stick a toothpick straight down into apple; slip neck onto toothpick. To set wings in place, first reconstruct apple. Place all wing sections back in their original positions, **then push sections of each wing back, separating them.** Make smallest wedge in top set stick up by cutting a little cross slit into second smallest wedge, then slip 1 end of smallest wedge into slit.

SWAN

1. Follow general method for duck. Position swan pattern so head is at narrow end of apple slice. Block cut it out, then saw cut pattern with paring knife. Trim fleshy side of beak to a point at skin side.

2. Make 3 primary wing sets as for duck, using the 6-inch knife. If there is room, make 2 or 3 tiny wedges in ribs of uncut apples between primary cavities, making 2 extra small wings for a more delicate look.

3. Mount head at narrow (flower) end of apple. Reconstruct apple and extend wings back from head.

Melon Duck & Melon Swan

INGREDIENTS: For each bird: 1 firm, fairly large cantaloupe, crenshaw or honeydew melon.

TOOLS & SUPPLIES: A paring knife, a knife with a blade that is longer than your melon, 2 wooden skewers, 1 small spoon plus melon duck and swan patterns on pages 139-141.

TIPS & TIMING: Duck: 10 minutes; swan, 20 minutes. Melons are easily bruised so handle cut pieces very carefully. Make them up a day ahead but store them with their wings unextended and tightly wrapped in plastic. You'll notice I don't put eyes on my ducks and swans. It's not that I'm lazy; I just like them that way. If you want to give yours a bird's eye view of your party, by all means do so. Use cloves or seeds from the fruit itself.

USE: Table-top centerpieces.

DUCK

1. **On a cutting board, hold melon with its stem end pointing straight up. You want to cut as large a slice as possible off 1 side but just miss seed pocket. Hold your blade over melon halfway between stem depression and side of melon. Cut straight down. This slice is 1/4 of width of melon.**

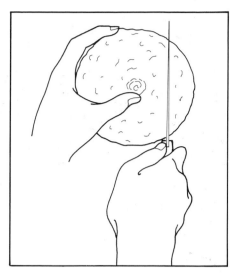

2. **Lay melon duck pattern onto flat side of this oval slice with beak pointing toward 1 end—the right end if you're right handed and to the left for left-handed persons. Lightly trace pattern with tip of your paring knife.** Remove and dry pattern. Cut most of excess melon away (block-cut around duck head design.) Hold your paring knife at a right angle to the flat side of the blocked-out slice and saw cut in from front of beak up over head and down back of neck. Now cut along bottom of beak and front of neck. Soften edges of duck's head with your paring knife.

3. With a small spoon, hollow out seed pocket. Clean it well, but don't scoop out any melon flesh.

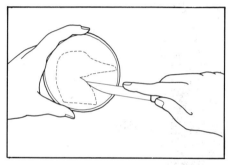

4. There are 3 sets of wings. They run along length of melon. Imagine stem end of melon is a clock face. The V-shaped set begins at 12 o'clock at top and center. The L-shaped side sets begin at 2:30 and 9:30. Do not cut any sets too deeply. The ribs in between wing cavities will be too thin to support top set of wings unless they are 1/2 inch thick. Stop short of middle of melon. You will probably cut into seed cavity by fourth wedge in your wing sets. No problem. These holes won't be visible in finished product. Make walls of wedges as thick as 2 nickels or thicker if your melon is extra large. Try to make 5 wedges per set.

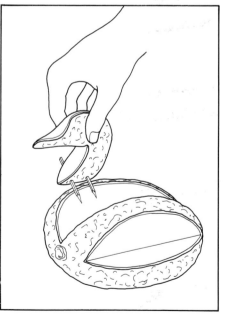

5. The head is set into front of top cavity opposite stem end. **Cut 1 pointed end off 2 wooden picks. Cut flesh side off bottom of neck forming a V that fits into bottom of cavity. Set neck in place. Pass your 2 pick points in first through flesh side near bottom of neck.** Angle picks so they pass across and down, going through melon skin nearer bottom of neck. Push them all the way in. Countersink picks with end of another wooden pick. Cover holes with a small, thin, melon slice so the duck doesn't look like its just been smooched by a vampire.

6. When setting top set of wings in place, be sure to put front end of largest wedge forward of hollow seed pocket. Tuck it right up against back of neck or it will fall in hole. Replace remainder of wings in usual manner.

SWAN

1. Follow general directions for melon duck.

2. Position swan's neck/head pattern lengthwise on oval slice. If the pattern is too long for the slice, then position it so that some of the bottom will extend down and disappear when the cutting begins (wouldn't it be great if dieting was that easy?) After tracing, block cut all around design. Trim beak to a point at skin side and round off edges all along head and neck. Cutting the underside of the neck is tricky. Don't try it in one single pass. First cut into the flesh to the depth of the skin. Now go over the first pass cutting through the skin. Trying to do it all in one pass often results in a slip and . . . a headless swan.

3. Make 3 primary wing sections just like melon duck. Now cut small sets (3 wedges per set) into ribs between primary cavities. You may also cut a small set below each primary side cavity. This makes 3 large wings and 4 small wings. Stay organized.

4. The swan's head is attached to whichever end of melon is more blunt. Cut your 2 skewers down to 2, pointed, 4-inch lengths. Push skewers into front of thick part of neck (lower middle) quite near skin. Place 1 skewer 1 inch above other. Hold back of neck against front of melon so its head is nice and high, then tap skewers into melon with side of your large knife. Countersink skewers so they don't show and cover holes with a *thin* slice of melon.

5. Place wings in standard manner but be sure to have smallest wedge in top sets sticking up. Remember, this is done by cutting a small slit into second-to-smallest wedge and inserting 1 end of smallest wedge into slit.

Raw vegetables can be served simply in a basket with dip or cut in bite-size pieces and arranged on a tray.

Kiwi Songbird

INGREDIENTS: 1 very firm, medium-size kiwifruit, 1 large red, black or green grape, 2 cloves, 1 (4-inch-long) pineapple leaf and 2 tiny leaves from center of pineapple.

TOOLS & SUPPLIES: A paring knife, 6-inch knife and 3 wooden picks.

TIPS & TIMING: Ask your grocer if you can take pineapple leaves. The answer is always a rather puzzled "Why, yes . . . " and you'll avoid expense of a whole pineapple. The songbird takes about 10 minutes to make and can be done 2 days ahead.

USES: A decorative and logical addition to the watermelon birdcage, the songbird also can be perched on shoulder of watermelon peacock or top of wishing well. You can also mount it on a small item such as half an orange and display it on a tray.

1. Body: With the 6-inch knife cut a V-shaped wing set (page 54), lengthwise down a narrow side of kiwifruit. Make just 3 wedges in this and following sets. This V-cut, narrow side is top of body. Make another L-shaped wing set on each wide side of body.

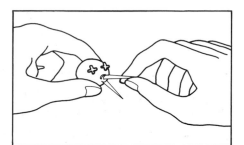

2. Head: Slice 1/3 off end of grape. Use bigger portion for the head. (A radish can also be used for head.) **Poke 2 holes into round end of grape for eyes and insert a clove in each hole. Cut blunt ends off 2 small pineapple leaves. The remaining leaf points make up bird's beak. Cut 2 horizontal slits in middle of round end of grape and slip blunt ends of leaves into slits.** The upper leaf should curve down on its sides; bottom leaf should curve up along its edges. Cut a thin slice off 1 end of kiwifruit so cut side of grape will fit flush against it. Insert 1 (or 2 for more stability) wooden pick into middle of kiwifruit through its cut end leaving 1/2 inch of wooden pick exposed. Slip head onto wooden pick and fit it flush against body.

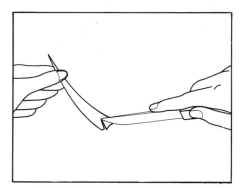

3. Tail: **Cut blunt end off large pineapple leaf so pointed end is 3 inches long. Cut a V-shaped notch into square end of this pointed section for the tail.** Cut a horizontal slit into end of kiwifruit and slip point of tail well into slit.

4. Mounting: Use 2 wooden picks for bird's legs. Push them into whatever base you're using and then slip bird's stomach onto upright wooden picks. Leave a little of legs exposed. Now set wings in their cavities, staggering wing sections back from head in normal fashion.

Pear Quail & Squash Goose

INGREDIENTS: For quail: 1 firm Bosc or Bartlett pear with a thick curving stem, 2 cloves, 1 nickel-sized carrot slice and some lemon juice in a saucer. For goose: 1 yellow crookneck squash with a fresh green stem, smooth skin and plump body, 2 cloves.

TOOLS & SUPPLIES: A paring knife, a 6-inch knife and 3 wooden picks.

TIPS & TIMING: Carve this design shortly before displaying it; lemon juice won't stop cut pear from browning for very long. The quail takes 5 minutes to cut. Each goose takes 3 minutes to carve. The wings dry out quickly, so make them up a few hours before the party, not earlier. If wings tend to fall out, stick them in place with a wooden pick half, covering point with small, outer wing section.

USES: A small centerpiece for platters during Christmas (as in "a partridge in a pear tree") holidays or on cheese boards anytime. Try displaying a cooing couple of quail together. While appearing on Gary Collin's TV show "Hour Magazine", I also made a covey of baby quail from those tiny Seckle pears and had them scurrying after their larger Bartlett pear Mom and Pop. Use geese for platter or table decorations.

PEAR QUAIL

1. Take a thin slice off bottom of pear so it stands leaning slightly in direction of curve of stem.

2. Eyes: Set 2 cloves near top under curve of stem.

3. Beak: Lay carrot slice flat and cut into its edge a quarter inch, splitting it open. Now, cut a narrow triangle down through slice, cutting the triangle tip in split side. Shorten beak by cutting off most of its solid, blunt side. Cut a horizontal slit into pear between and just under eyes. Slip beak, blunt end first, into slit and open beak with edge of knife blade.

4. Wings: **Make a set of L-shaped wings on right and left side of body. Start smallest wedge in each set about 1/2 inch above fattest part of body. Cut down 1/2 inch or so. Now, cut straight in from side at level of bottom of that vertical cut. This makes first wedge in set.** All successive wedges have walls a little thicker than a nickel. Make 5 wedges per set but stop sooner if you are beginning to cut off sides of head. After dipping wings in lemon juice, place them back on pear and stagger their sections to rear of body.

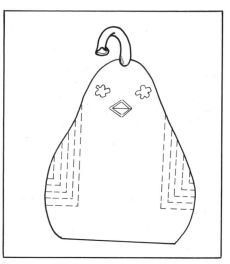

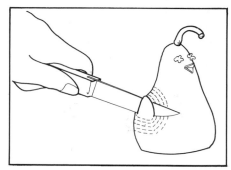

SQUASH GOOSE

1. Beak: **Pare stem into a point that angles down. Cut a horizontal notch into front of beak to open it, if you like.**

2. Eyes: Insert a clove into top of squash just above and behind beak; 1 on each side.

3. Wings: Cut 3 L-shaped wedges out of each side of body. Make these down in fat part of squash. They are just like pear quail's wings. Use your 6-inch knife to do cutting, and wait until later to put wings in place.

4. Legs: Cut 1 end off 2 wooden picks. Split blunt ends of wooden picks with point of your paring knife. Make 4 toes by first cutting down through top of blunt end, then give pick a quarter turn and cut through again. Spread split ends. Insert pointed ends of picks into belly of squash. Adjust depth of picks so squash stands on tripod consisting of its bottom and 2 wooden picks, leaning forward a little.

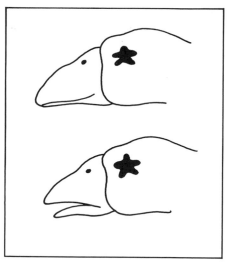

Watermelon Baskets

Give a cool spring or summer look to any brunch, bridal or baby shower, buffet, tea or dinner party table with these fabulous watermelon works of art. They are guaranteed to become conversation pieces. And they only take about 30 minutes to create.

Watermelon Birdcage

INGREDIENTS: 1 evenly shaped, rather long, oval, room temperature watermelon.

TOOLS & SUPPLIES: Paring knife, 6-inch knife, chef's knife, scoring tool, scissors or garden shears, spoon, bamboo skewer and metal skewer or icepick.

TIPS & TIMING: The cage takes about 25 minutes to carve. Make it a day ahead. Store wrapped in plastic and refrigerate. If mounting kiwi songbird on crossbar, first push 2 wooden picks for bird's legs into crossbar before putting crossbar in place. See Tips for Watermelon Baskets, page 20.

USES: A free-standing table decoration at brunches, spring weddings and summer picnics.

1. Use more dome-shaped end of melon for top of cage. Cut a few inches off other end so melon stands flat.

2. The cuts in steps 3 and 4 are all made in 2 stages. The first stage consists of cutting lines of design skin deep—no more than 1/4 inch deep, using paring knife held in a pencil grip. In second stage, deepen cuts with the 6-inch knife. If you try to cut deeply without first etching design you will probably split melon.

3. There are no front bars on cage. **Therefore, cut out and remove upper 2/3 of half the melon.**

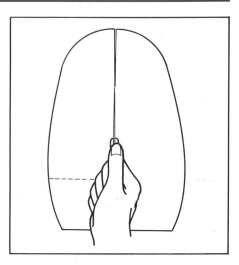

4. This leaves back half of upper part of melon with which to make vertical bars, simulating a cage. **This is done by carving out long vertical triangles leaving vertical bars in place. The triangles taper to points about 1 inch out from center of top. They do not meet.** The very top of melon is left whole, joining bars of cage together. The 1-inch-wide triangles actually have parallel, vertical sides. The bars should be about 1 inch wide too. The number of bars depends on size of melon; 6 or 7 will do. Be sure bars at front of each side are straight and strong. Use your knife as much as possible to trim inside of bars straight, leaving a little pink flesh on rind. Use spoon to get at less accessible areas, hollowing out top of cage.

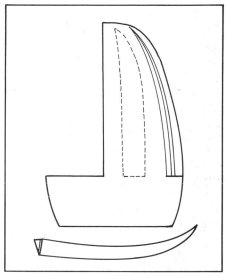

5. Use 1 of the vertical wedges to make crossbar. Cut it to a length 1 inch more than distance between 2 front sides of cage at a point halfway up bars. Trim crossbar so it is even along its length. **Cut a notch out of inside of each of 2 front vertical bars so crossbar will snugly fit into sides, going across cage about half way up.**

6. With icepick or metal skewer, poke a hole through outside of vertical front bars in middle of notches. Now pass skewer through crossbar, lengthwise, making a hole clear through it.

7. Remove metal skewer. Run wooden skewer through hole in crossbar. Thread wooden skewer through hole in 1 notch (from inside) and seat that end of crossbar into notch. Swing other end of crossbar into place. Now tap skewer back into second upright bar to give support to both sides. Trim off any exposed skewer with your scissors or garden shears.

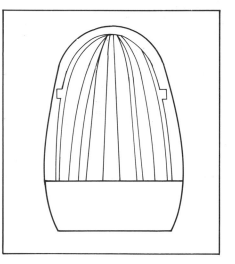

8. Use your scoring tool to make a diamond pattern (or simple crosshatching) all around bottom of cage. Hollow out some of fruit from bottom of cage and fill cavity with fruit salad garnished with mint leaves, or put a bird's nest of alfalfa sprouts on cage bottom and lay in a few grapes, melon balls or kumquats for eggs.

Watermelon Baby Carriage

INGREDIENTS: 1 large, room temperature watermelon, 1 end noticeably larger than other, 1 pink grapefruit and 4 cucumber ends.

TOOLS & SUPPLIES: A paring knife, 6-inch and 9-inch knives, zester and/or scoring tool, wooden picks and a spoon.

TIPS & TIMING: Carving time is about 20 minutes. Attach handle just before displaying carriage. You can also make cabbage angel, page 112, minus halo and wings and put it in carriage. See Tips for Watermelon Baskets, page 20.

USES: A fruit salad bowl at a baby shower or infant's birthday party.

1. Hold melon so it is resting upright on 1 end. With 9-inch knife, cut a 1/4-inch-thick slice off least attractive side of melon. Rest melon on its cut side.

2. **With your paring knife, etch outline of shaded area in drawing into upper part of melon. Notice handle is at narrower end.** Deepen etched outline with 6-inch knife. Cut melon inside outline into smaller sections and remove these sections.

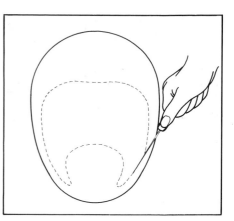

3. **Now cut U-shaped section off narrow end.** Trim off most of flesh from inside of this piece leaving just a hint of pink on rind. Carve out center of this piece, thus creating handle for carriage.

4. Hollow out carriage by first slicing down along inside of its sides and canopy with your paring knife, then scoop out flesh with your spoon. Leave 2 inches of melon intact at bottom. **Cut V's or waves along edges of canopy and sides but leave area where handle was removed smooth.**

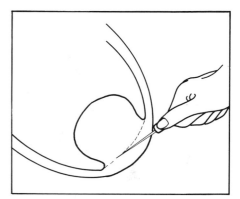

5. Wheels: Cut 4 (1/2-inch-thick) slices crosswise from grapefruit for wheels. **Attach them with a wooden pick half per wheel passed through pithy top edge of each slice.** For hubcaps, push a wooden pick half through center of each wheel and 1/2 inch into melon. Slip fleshy side of a cucumber end onto exposed blunt end of pick and press it onto wheel. End cuts from limes, oranges or red radishes may be substituted for cucumbers. For hubcaps in the old fifties flipper style, use red radish rosettes (page 32).

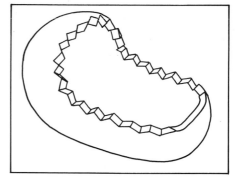

6. Attach handle by inserting 3 wooden picks halfway into melon near skin. Press handle onto exposed wooden picks.

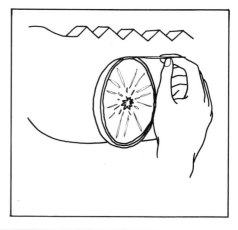

Watermelon Peacock

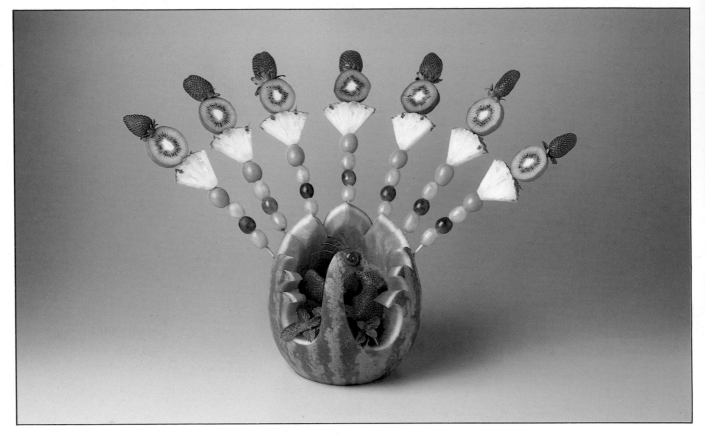

INGREDIENTS: 1 large, oval, room temperature watermelon, maraschino cherries with stems, 1 small orange chili or yellow chili, 7 strawberries, 7 kumquats, 7 red grapes, 14 green grapes, 2 (1/2-inch thick) pineapple slices, 2 firm kiwifruit. This is not a cheap design!

TOOLS & SUPPLIES: Paring knife, 6-inch and 9-inch knives, peacock pattern on page 139, adhesive tape, spoon, wooden picks and 7 (10-inch) wooden skewers.

TIPS & TIMING: It takes 45 minutes to carve melon and skewer fruit. The melon can be carved 3 days in advance but do not make up skewers more than 1 day ahead. Store skewers on a cookie tray, wrapped in plastic and refrigerated. Attach them without strawberries just before displaying peacock. Set berries in place after skewers are inserted into melon.

USES: As a centerpiece at any party celebrating something to be proud of. Fill cavity with mint leaves and your leftover berries. Surround it with fruit salad or fruit skewers.

1. Slice stem end off melon with your large knife. Stand melon on its cut end. **Tape peacock pattern onto smoothest and most evenly colored side so bottom of neck is 4 to 5 inches above bottom of melon. With tip of your paring knife, etch design just through surface of skin.**

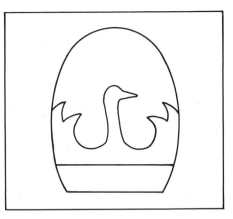

2. Turn melon around so its beak faces away from you. Stick a wooden pick into each end of your etched side wings. This simply makes it easier to locate these points as you etch back of melon. Locate center point between wooden picks. Near top of melon, directly above center point, etch a center peak and, as pictured, etch 3 more peaks on each side going down until you reach wooden picks. If the peaks don't come out evenly spaced, it's OK. It's a bird, not a rocket ship—it need not be perfectly symmetrical. Remove pattern and wooden picks.

3. Using a gentle sawing motion, deepen etched design with your paring knife. Cut no deeper than 1 inch into melon and hold knife so it aims into middle of melon's core as you proceed. Go back over pattern again, cutting in as far as possible with your paring knife. Now deepen your cuts with 6-inch knife where possible. Cut area inside design into small sections and remove them. Cut along inner face of melon so its walls will be 1 inch thick. Neatly hollow out melon with a spoon leaving about 3 inches of flesh intact at bottom. Trim neck and beak smooth.

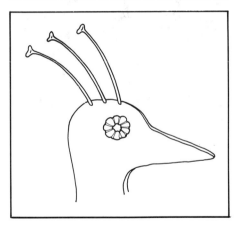

4. **Eye: Use a maraschino cherry half or a slice crosscut from stem end of a chili.** Attach eye with a wooden pick point.

5. **Head feathers: Pull stems out of 3 or more maraschino cherries. Leave fruit end of stem alone and cut off thick portion of other end. Pierce top of head with a wooden pick in 3 or more places as shown and slip cut end of each stem into holes.**

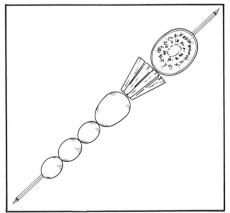

6. Tail Feathers: Cut kiwifruit into slices 1/3 inch thick. Cut pineapple into 1/2-inch-thick triangular wedges. Trim tip off each triangle. **Starting with kiwifruit, arrange fruit onto 7 skewers as shown.** You may substitute melon balls for grapes and kumquats. Attach skewers by pushing each 1 in through back of melon 1 inch or so under each peak. Push them down at an almost vertical angle. Cap each skewer with a strawberry.

7. If you have a very sharp, small melon baller or a U-shaped wood-carving gouge, you can cut out a pattern of feathers from peacock's breast before attaching skewers. For each feather, make a short cut almost straight into skin; make another cut 1/2 inch below first one. Cut out a wedge between the 2 cuts. You can use scoring tools or zester to etch feathers into skin as well.

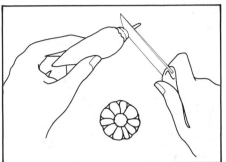

Watermelon Wishing Well

INGREDIENTS: 1 long, cylinder-shaped, room temperature watermelon, 1 (2-inch) carrot section and 1 cucumber end.

TOOLS & SUPPLIES: Paring knife, 6-inch and 9-inch knives, scoring tool, spoon, long metal skewer or ice pick, 1 (10-inch) wooden skewer and 1 wooden pick.

TIPS & TIMING: The well takes 20 minutes to carve. It can be made 1 day ahead. See Tips for Watermelon Baskets, page 20.

USES: A picnic table centerpiece. Perfect for springtime brunches and wedding receptions.

1. Use more evenly dome-shaped end for top of well. With large knife, cut 1 to 2 inches off other end. Rest melon on its cut side.

2. Study drawing. **The middle arch is 1-1/2 inches wide. Etch lines into skin with your paring knife. Deepen cuts with 6-inch knife and remove these sections.** Cut flesh out of remaining arch leaving a little pink showing.

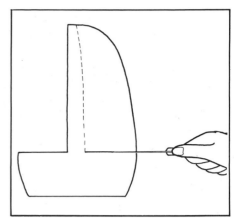

3. Cut around inside of bottom so its circular wall will be 1 inch thick. Scoop flesh out of bottom with a spoon. Leave 2 inches of melon flesh intact at bottom.

4. **With scoring tool, cut out 3 or more parallel, horizontal strips of skin from around base.** Save 1 strip—it will be rope for well's bucket. With your paring knife, cut small grooves around top of base. These denote ends of bricks. **With your scoring tool, complete a brick pattern around outside of base, as pictured.**

5. Cut a crossbar out of 1 of large sections removed in step 2. This bar should match upright arch in thickness and be 1 inch longer than distance between uprights at a point about halfway up.

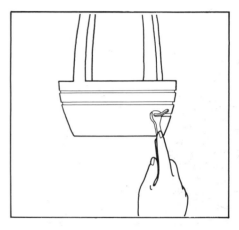

6. Hold crossbar horizontally up against back of uprights just a little higher than half way up. Mark each upright where bar rests against it at both top and bottom. Set bar down and cut out a 1/2-inch-deep recession from inside of each upright just between your marks.

7. Run a metal skewer straight through crossbar lengthwise. Remove it and pierce holes through melon's skin just behind each of recessed notches. Cut blunt end off wooden skewer so its length is 1/2 inch longer than distance between outsides of uprights. Pass pointed end of wood skewer into pierced hole in 1 upright. Hold crossbar so you can feed skewer through hole in it. Pass skewer through crossbar. Set loose end of crossbar in its notch and tap skewer all way in with side of your large knife.

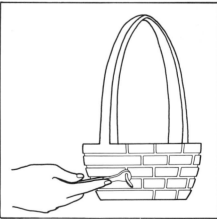

8. **Cut carrot into a 1/4-inch-thick rectangular block. Pare handle out from this block, as pictured. Smooth handle's edges and fit it onto exposed skewer point.**

9. Tuck 1 end of "rope" into joint where upright and crossbar meet. Loop rope around bar a few times. Let its loose end fall down into well.

10. Hollow out a 1- to 2-inch long end piece from a cucumber. Make thin V-cuts down its sides to simulate wooden slats. Pass a wooden pick into top of bucket, pierce end of rope and pass pick through other side of bucket. Set bucket on top of "bricks."

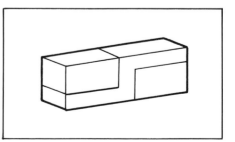

Special Designs

Whether elegant or whimsical, garnishes and centerpieces set the theme for a festive event. Most of these take about 20 minutes to prepare (some require additional soaking in cold water to firm up) and they can be prepared up to 3 days ahead.

Melon Swan Fruit Bowl

INGREDIENTS: A large, firm melon—crenshaw, honeydew, Persian or cantaloupe, at room temperature.

TOOLS & SUPPLIES: A paring knife, soup spoon and swan fruit bowl pattern on page 140.

TIPS & TIMING: Use patterns as a guide but feel free to vary designs. The number of curving peaks that represent side wings can be increased or decreased to suit your taste. The bowl can be made 3 days ahead. It takes 20 minutes to carve.

USES: Fill bowl with raspberries, blueberries or small strawberries. It makes a very special serving container. The bowl can also be used to hold a honey-yogurt dip for fruit skewers, grapes or strawberries.

1. **Cut a small slice off shoulder of broader end of melon.** Rest it on this cut side.

2. Hold (or tape) pattern on melon as shown. The base of swan's neck is at lower, broader end of melon. Etch patterned design into melon, skin deep. The pattern only covers neck, head and right side of swan. After tracing these, reverse pattern, laying it along left side with bottom of neck back in same place. Trace side wing portion of pattern onto left side of melon, disregarding head and upper neck (unless you want a 2-headed swan, and, in this case, 2 heads are really not better than 1!).

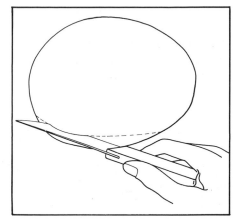

3. Remove pattern. Stick a wooden pick into ends of traced lines on both sides of melon just to mark these spots. Now etch a series of 3 or more peaks around back of melon. The series can rise in middle or be split like a swallow's tail. To balance layout of these back peaks, it's best to start in middle and work back to each wooden pick, 1 side at a time.

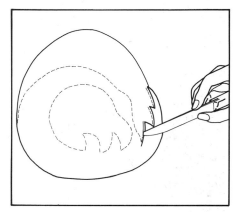

4. Remove wooden picks. **Now go back over etched design cutting it deeper into center.** Cut extraneous pieces away in small sections. Scoop out seeds with a spoon.

5. **Trim head and neck, giving a rounded curve to their undersides.** Also cut down around interior about 1/2 inch in from melon skin so interior walls are straight and cleanly defined. Now scoop out excess flesh below this cut with a spoon.

Eggheads, Chicks & Bunnies

INGREDIENTS: Hard-boiled eggs plus: **Eggheads:** Ripe olives, hard salami slices, wilted green onion leaves, canned pimiento, red radishes and cloves; **Bunnies:** 3 cloves and a tiny piece of cauliflower; **Chicks:** 2 cloves and a 2-inch carrot length.

TOOLS & SUPPLIES: A paring knife and wooden picks.

TIPS & TIMING: You can boil eggs a few days ahead, but decorate them the day they will be displayed.

USES: The chicks and bunnies are for Easter parties. The eggheads can be dressed to accent platters with a variety of ethnic themes and on deviled egg trays any time.

EGGHEADS

1. Cut a thin slice off wide end of egg and stand egg on that end. **Cut a smile into top 1/3 of egg. The top lip is made with an horizontal cut. The bottom lip angles back up into top.** Remove piece between cuts.

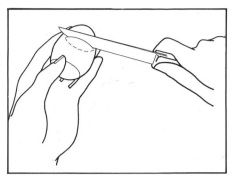

2. Hats: Insert tip of your knife into center of a salami slice and cut out through edge. Draw 1 end of cut edge over other. This will form a cone shape for an Oriental hat. To make a sombrero, fold bottom edge of cone up into a brim. You can make a variety of traditional hats by fooling around with brim shape. Secure your hat by piercing salami with a wooden pick.

3. Clothes: Belts, suspenders, bikinis, bandanas and neckerchiefs can be made with wilted green onion leaves (boiled 10 seconds) or strips of canned pimentos. Bow ties, buttons, arms and feet are made with ripe olives. Small pieces will stick to eggs. Large pieces must be attached with wooden pick points.

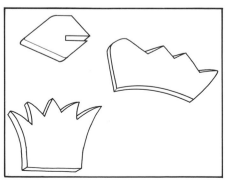

BUNNIES

1. **Lengthwise, cut a 1/4-inch-thick slice off 1 side of egg as shown in second drawing and rest egg on its cut side.**

2. **Cut bottom slice in half lengthwise.** These are bunny ears. Insert a wooden pick halfway into the egg where each ear should be. Slip each ear onto a wooden pick.

3. For eyes, insert a small clove into egg just in front of each ear. Use a large clove at very front for nose. Slip a wooden pick into stem of a small caulifloweret and set it into back of egg for bunny tail.

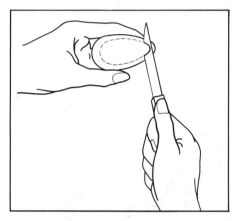

CHICKS

1. Follow step 1 for bunny.

2. **Cut 2 carrot strips from the 2-inch carrot piece, about as thick as a nickel. Trim these pieces into a cock's comb, tail and beak as shown.**

3. Make a horizontal slit into wide end of egg and insert tail piece. Cut another slit down center of top of narrow end and insert cock's comb there. Cut a hole into very front of narrow end and insert beak. Use 2 small cloves for eyes.

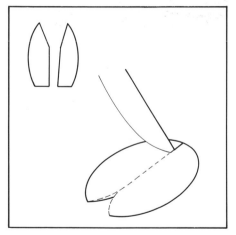

Jícama Bunny

INGREDIENTS: 1/2 jícama, cut from stem to root, 1 Belgian endive (or small Napa cabbage leaves), 1 red radish, 1 ripe olive, 1 green onion root and 1 small caulifloweret.

TOOLS & SUPPLIES: A paring knife, 6-inch knife, vegetable peeler and wooden picks.

TIPS & TIMING: Carving body takes 20 minutes. Brush it with lemon juice if you make it a few days ahead. The ears wilt after being on display for 2 hours, giving bunny an amusing, floppy-eared look. Unless you are an accomplished sculptor, don't try to whittle jícama into a highly detailed bunny. An over-carved bunny looks like a frog. If you are an adept sculptor, carve bunny standing up on its haunches, its head held high. The following instructions yield a crouching bunny.

USES: A table decoration during Easter season and on buffets featuring rabbit.

1. Lay jícama half on its flat side. **With the 6-inch knife, peel and trim it into an egg shape with a flat bottom.** The head will be at narrow end. **With your fingernail or end of vegetable peeler, scrape a groove on each side of top at narrow end (1).** This creates ridge of nose. Narrow front of face but leave puffy cheeks.

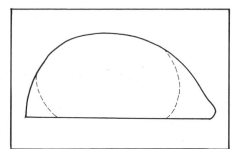

2. **Cut a 1/2-inch-deep horizontal notch at extreme lower part of narrow end (2).** This separates head from front paws. Extend notch around sides of head to create an illusion of forearms. Round off bottom of head. Cut a notch out of front to separate paws.

3. The right hind leg has shape of a number 2. The left leg is a 2 in reverse. **Shape legs by first cutting 2's 1/4 inch deep into sides of wide end (3).** Now whittle some of jícama away from top and front of 2's. **Round off edges of hind legs and cut a small notch in front of each paw to define them (4).**

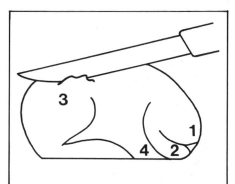

4. Eyes: Cut 2 round slices off side of red radish. Attach them, skin side up, using wooden pick points. For pupils, cut 2 tiny round slices from side of a ripe olive and attach them to tips of wooden picks.

5. Whiskers: Poke 3 holes into each side of nose. Insert a single strand of green onion root into each hole.

6. Tail: Insert a wooden pick half into stem of caulifloweret and stick it into top of wide end.

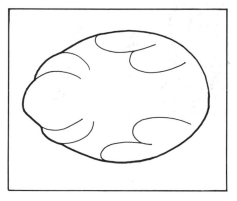

7. Ears: Trim bottoms of 2 Belgian endive leaves so they fit flush on top of head behind eyes. To attach them, insert a wooden pick half into each side of head, point up. Let 1/2 inch of each point remain exposed. Slip bottom of each leaf onto points.

Cauliflower Lamb

INGREDIENTS: 5 cauliflower heads, 1 rather thin eggplant, 1 (2-inch) section of wide end of a carrot, 1 red radish, 1 green grape, 3 ounces lemon juice and salt.

TOOLS & SUPPLIES: A paring knife, 6-inch knife, wooden picks, Styrofoam, pastry brush and a saucer.

TIPS & TIMING: Once you have core of styrofoam completed, lamb takes 1 to 2 hours to assemble. Yes—2 Hours! It's a real food sculpting marathon. However the core can be used over and over and the lamb keeps well for 3 days if brushed with lemon juice.

USES: The perfect centerpiece for Easter brunch and on buffets featuring lamb.

1. **The lamb is built on a Styrofoam core 8 inches long, 4 inches wide and 5 to 6 inches high. It is rounded off along sides of top like a loaf of bread.** Use a single piece of foam, if possible. If craft stores near you only sell thin sheets of foam, you can still construct a block suitable for carving into bread loaf shape. Spread liquid glue onto sheets you are joining. Stick wooden picks halfway into 1 sheet of foam and then press 2 sheets together. When set, carve glued block into loaf shape.

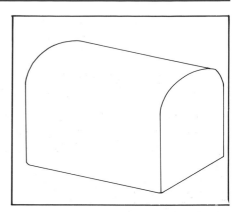

2. Head: Cut a 4-inch piece off wide end of eggplant. Insert 5 wooden picks halfway into 1 end of foam in a 2-inch-wide circle. Push cut side of eggplant end piece onto wooden picks, then push it up against foam. Stick a wooden pick into stem of a large caulifloweret and attach it to opposite end of foam to counterbalance piece, otherwise it will fall on its face.

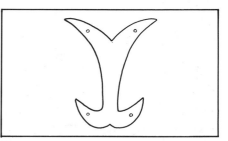

3. **Nose: From carrot section, cut out a center slice 2 inches long, 1-1/2 inches wide and 1/8 inch thick. Carve this slice into shape of an anchor, as shown, to make the nose.** Put it in a saucer and salt it heavily. The salt will soften the carrot while you make up rest of lamb.

4. Lamb's wool: Cut individual caulifloweret stems short. **Slip a wooden pick (or a wooden pick half cut on diagonal for smaller pieces) into stem, then stick into foam. Attach them 1 at a time. Frame head with small cauliflowerets first.** Then fill in space below head, working your way back around sides behind head. Fit pieces close together.

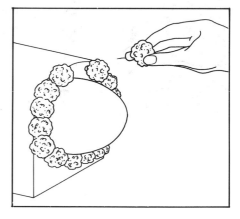

5. **Ears: These are cut from leftover eggplant. They are shaped like tiny guitar bodies, 3 inches long.** Leave up to 1/4 inch flesh attached to skin. Brush flesh with lemon juice to keep it white. Attach ears, skin sides up, with 2 wooden picks passed through top of each ear. Cover ends of wooden picks with cauliflower.

6. Cover remainder of body with cauliflowerets.

7. Face: Rinse salted nose. Insert a wooden pick point into each corner of anchor-shaped nose. Press nose onto front of head. Make eyes by first cutting 2 thin cross sections from radish. Stick 1 onto each side of head with a wooden pick point, leaving a little of point exposed. Cover each point with half of a green grape.

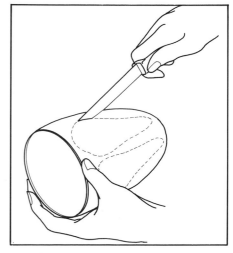

Butterfly

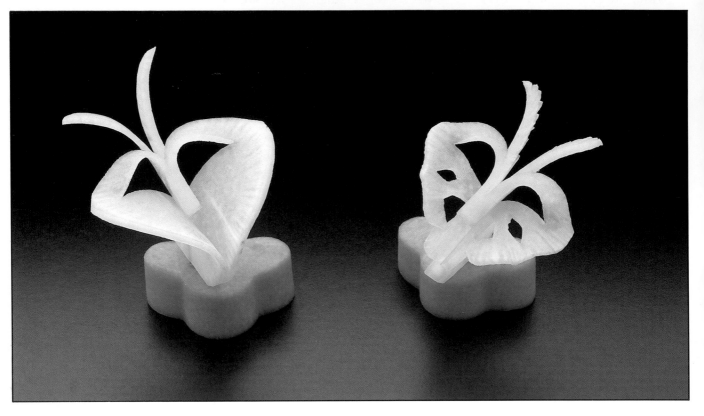

INGREDIENTS: 1 (3-inch) Daikon radish section (or a thick carrot, turnip, rutabaga, cucumber or beet).

TOOLS & SUPPLIES: A 6-inch knife, paring knife and wooden pick.

TIPS & TIMING: The basic butterfly takes less than 1 minute. Soak the opened butterfly in cold water for only 5 minutes. This will firm it. Oversoaking will close wings.

USES: As garnishes on serving trays and accents on salads. You can attach them to watermelon wells, cages and baskets and include them in vegetable flower bouquets.

1. Up to 10 butterflies can be made from 1 (3-inch) Daikon radish section. The thickness of wings varies. If your radish is 3 inches wide, slices for wings can be 1/8 inch thick. If you use a small carrot, then wings should be as thin as a dime.

2. There are only 5 cuts to basic design. Lay radish on its side. The first cut is a slice off 1 end that stops at a point about 80 percent of way down through radish. The second cut is parallel to first slice and of equal thickness, however, it goes all way down. You now have a set of wings, joined at bottom.

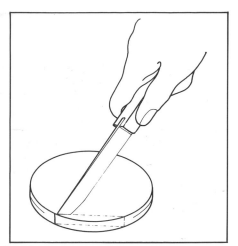

3. Lay this wing set down. Imagine it's a clockface, opened at 12 and joined at 6. **The third cut is a very small slice taken off bottom, between 5:30 and 6:30.**

4. **The feelers are made with fourth cut. It goes through both layers. Cut in at 12:00 and follow curve of radish down to 4:00. You should end this cut 1/4 inch in from edge of radish. Withdraw blade.**

5. **The last and fifth cut also goes through both layers. It starts inside feeler cut by 1/4 inch and runs parallel to it, coming out of bottom at 5:30.**

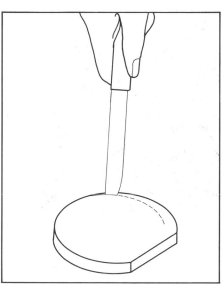

6. Gently separate wings and lift bottom of feelers up. Tuck bottom of feelers in between wings. Spread feelers open.

7. Insert a wooden pick into bottom of butterfly and mount it on a small pedestal, such as end of a cucumber.

8. After you are familiar with position of feeler cut you can make this design more delicate by cutting notches out of edge of radish just in front of where feeler cut will be made. Then make feeler cut and last cut. Before you open wings, cut small holes through them and trim edges of wings to your liking.

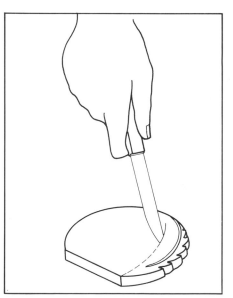

Red-Combed Rooster

INGREDIENTS: 2 firm cantaloupes, 1 red bell pepper (or pimiento), 1 acorn (Table Queen) squash, 2 chilies, preferably red but orange will suffice.

TOOLS & SUPPLIES: Paring knife, 6- and 9-inch knives, zester, melon baller, wooden pick and 6 wood skewers.

TIPS & TIMING: The rooster takes 30 minutes to cut and assemble. It keeps well for 3 days.

USES: As a table decoration for buffets featuring chicken.

1. Body: Cut a 1/2-inch-thick slice off least attractive side of melon and rest it on this cut side.

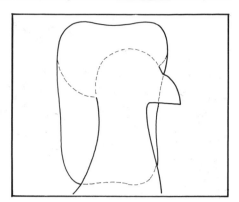

2. Head: Cut 1 side off second melon. This slice should be 1/4 of width of whole melon. Lay rooster head pattern (page 141) on slice so beak is close to edge of slice. Trace pattern and cut out head with your paring knife. Round off top of beak and, if you wish, leave it as is. Otherwise, cut a half inch section off tip of red chili. Hollow it out. Pare beak so chili will fit over it. Secure chili beak with a wooden pick point sticking out of front of pared melon beak.

3. Eyes: Cut a crosswise slice from stem end of 2 chilies as shown for peacock, page 71. The slices should include a little flesh but be primarily composed of base of stems. Secure eyes with wooden pick points.

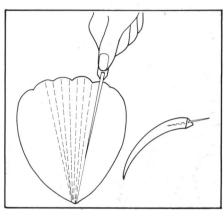

4. Comb & Wattles: First insert 2 parallel, upright 6-inch skewers into front of melon. Slip head down onto skewers. **Now cut a slice off 1 side of bell pepper. Be sure to cut down near stem so slice has a rounded top. Hold slice behind top of rooster head so 1 inch or more of top of slice is visible.** Etch outline of top of head into slice. Now cut off top of slice along your etched line, thus creating comb. Cut a wooden pick in half on a diagonal. Push wooden pick halves into bottom of comb, then press comb onto head. If desired, from remainder of pepper slice cut 2 guitar-shaped pieces each about 1 inch wide and 2 inches long. Press dull end of a wooden pick point into fleshy side of top of each "guitar." Angle points down and stick each wattle into opposite sides of head just behind beak.

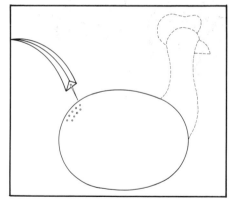

5. Tail Feathers: Cut squash in half. Also cut in half remainder of melon from which you made head. Scoop seeds out of squash and melon halves with a melon baller or spoon. **Cut squash into 7 or 8 slices that are each 1/2 inch wide at stem end but pointed at opposite end.** Cut slices that also have a wedged and pointed shape from across width of melon half. Taper flesh from slices as shown. **Insert a whole wooden pick into thick end of each piece and set them into back of melon body in 3 rows of 5 feathers per row, again, as pictured.**

6. Side Wings: **Take 2 full surface slices off remainder of squash.** With your zester, etch a feathered pattern into skin of each slice. Hollow both slices using your melon baller in a scraping motion. Set 2 wooden picks into each slice and press each into opposite sides of body.

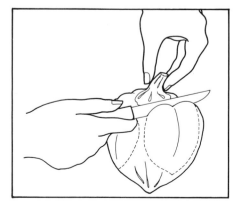

Flying Fruit Kites

INGREDIENTS: 1 watermelon end piece, 1 red apple, 1 green apple, 1 lemon, 1 orange, 1 lime, lemon juice and carrot leaf stems.

TOOLS & SUPPLIES: A paring knife, 10- and 12-inch bamboo skewers (or thin metal florist's rods.)

TIPS & TIMING: Each kite takes 3 to 5 minutes to carve. They keep 2 days.

USES: As table decorations for picnics, patio parties and children's parties.

1. Cut 1 or more slices off sides of apples and citrus fruit. Make these about 3 inches long, 2 inches wide and 1/4-inch thick in middle.

2. **Trim slices into diamond shapes. Cut away any fruity pulp from insides of citrus pieces.** You can now leave diamond-shaped kites as is or cut a cross pattern into fleshy inside of each kite. If you etch in cross pattern, pare flesh from around pattern, leaving kite's cross intact.

3. Use watermelon end as a base from which to fly kites. Substitute any large food item for melon, if you wish. Set melon base on its flat side. Bend 6 or more skewers into gentle arcs and stick them into base, points up.

4. Pierce bottom of each kite with point of a skewer. Strip leaves from carrot tops so leaf stems are bare. **Into hole at bottom of each kite insert thicker end of a carrot stem to make tails.**

5. Push fleshy underside of each kite onto point of each skewer. Have them all facing in same general direction.

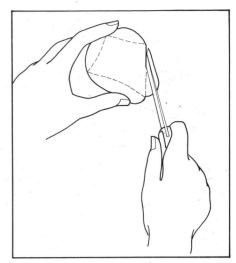

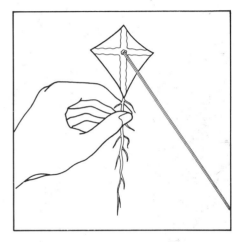

Sweet Potato Seal & Walrus

INGREDIENTS: 1 sweet potato per seal or walrus, 2 cloves per design, plus green onion roots, a few bean sprouts, 1 round red radish and lemon juice.

TOOLS & SUPPLIES: Paring knife, vegetable peeler, pastry brush and wooden picks.

TIPS & TIMING: Carving time is 10 to fifteen minutes each. Brush potatoes with lemon juice to prevent browning. These designs keep for 3 days. The key to these designs is in selection of potatoes. Shop around for some whose shape clearly resembles that of a seal or walrus.

USES: Table or platter decorations for parties at sea coast.

1. Peel skin from potatoes but leave a small bit intact at tip of nose. Use peeler to shape body. Usually tail area needs to be reduced in size somewhat. **Use paring knife to cut creases across back of a sea lion or walrus to denote rolls of fat if you like.** Brush with lemon juice before proceeding.

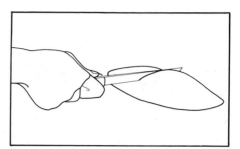

2. **Use paring knife to cut 4 flippers for each seal. All flipper cuts start near middle of stomach. The front flippers go toward head, then up sides of chest. The rear flippers go back along bottom, then come up on back on each side. The flippers are no thicker than a nickel, or thinner if you can manage it—they are prone to cracking. If they break off just lean them against body when you display finished piece.**

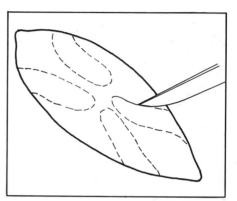

3. Bend cut flippers away from body and slice stomach area flat. The flippers do not actually hold these designs in position—they rest on flat stomach cut.

4. For eyes, poke 2 holes in head with wooden pick, then insert a clove into each hole. Use 2 short bean sprouts for walrus tusks. Insert them into wooden pick holes. Substitute wooden pick halves for sprouts if you wish. Whiskers of green onion roots can be inserted into tiny holes made on both sides of face or simply attach a section of green onion root to each side with a wooden pick point. If your seal has its head pointing up, balance a red radish ball on its nose with another wooden pick point.

Daikon Radish Sailboats

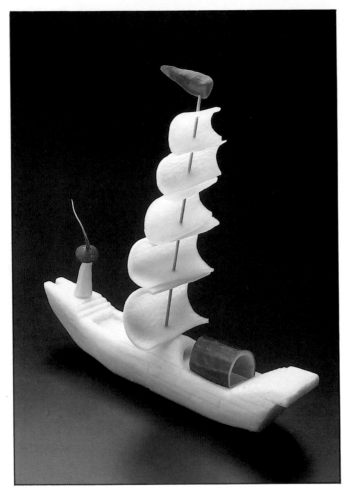

INGREDIENTS: 2 Daikon radishes, 1 straight radish and 1 slightly curved like a banana, both 3 inches wide and at least 1 foot long, 1 thick carrot or cucumber, 1 small red radish and 1 small, fresh chili.

TOOLS & SUPPLIES: Paring knife, 6- and 9-inch knives, vegetable peeler, a 10-inch wood skewer and 1 wooden pick.

TIPS & TIMING: The carving can take 45 minutes or more, depending on details you carve into ship. It keeps well for 3 days. When carving sails, be sure radish is up to room temperature.

USES: As a table decoration for parties having a nautical theme or for parties that feature seafood.

1. There is no 1 correct sailboat design. When carving hull (body of boat) use curved radish. Begin by cutting a thin, straight slice off convex side so radish sits flat. Feel free to carve any hull design: a Spanish galleon, racing schooner, Chinese junk, or clipper ship for example. Carving the Oriental design will enable you to carve any other type of boat since this design includes the basic steps.

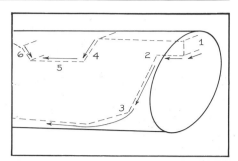

2. **Using 6-inch knife, make sequence of cuts as shown in drawing. Note they are all straight cuts.** Next, use 9-inch knife to shape front and sides of hull. Smooth hull with your vegetable peeler.

3. Steps: Start at top of slopes created by cuts 4 and 9. Cut down 1/4 inch, lift knife out, then cut in horizontally at bottom of vertical cut so 2 cuts meet. This makes 1 step. Repeat this two-cut process starting at front of top step and cutting steps down face of slope.

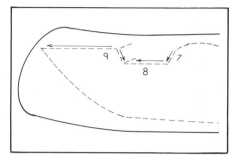

4. **To hollow out an area for a ship's hold, or to recess an area around a cabin, first cut border of area 1/4 inch deep or more with paring knife in a pencil grip. Next make shallow crosscuts within border wherever you plan to have a recessed area.** Use tip of your vegetable peeler to gouge out crosshatched little squares.

5. You can etch a pattern of wood planking into hull using your fingernail or cut design by making thin, continuous V-cuts.

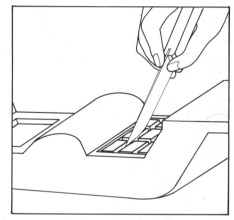

6. Sails: Peel second radish and crosscut it into 3 sections 4 or 5 inches long. **A sail is made by cutting a little more than halfway around side of each section, as shown in drawing. Use a gentle sawing motion turning radish into blade.** The sails should be at least as thick as a nickel. You'll be cutting directly toward your hand. It's potentially rather dangerous. Do yourself a favor and protect your hand by holding the radish with a thick cloth as you cut. Three or more sails can be made from each section. Once you have number of sails you want, set your skewer(s) straight down into hull, blunt end first. Sink these "masts" all way to bottom of hull. Now slip sails onto mast with largest sail at bottom. Once all sails are in place, pull sails and mast out as a unit, lay it down and trim edges.

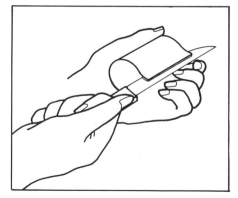

7. Canopy & Deckhands: Make a "sail" from thick end of the carrot. Use a cucumber or zucchini as a substitute. Its length should match length of recessed area it will cover. Fit canopy into recess in deck, as pictured. For an Oriental deckhand, push a wooden pick part way into deck. Cut stem end from chili and push chili onto wooden pick. Cap chili with a slice from root end of red radish.

8. Store boat hull and sails as 2 units. Before wrapping sails in plastic, let them rest (on mast) in a sink of cool water for 5 minutes. This firms them up. Use any little scraps of food to make small flags for tops of masts.

Carrot Fishing Net

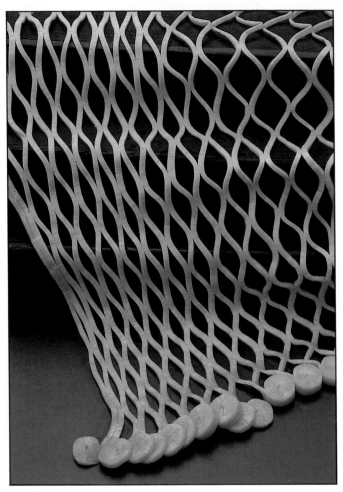

INGREDIENTS: 1 (4-inch) carrot length at least 1-1/2 inches wide, 1/2 cup salt and 2 cups water at room temperature.

TOOLS & SUPPLIES: 6-inch knife, ice pick, wood skewer and a small bowl.

TIPS & TIMING: Soaking time to soften carrot is at least 8 hours. Then cutting takes 10 minutes per net. Shop around for very fat carrots. The fatter the carrot the longer the net will be. Finished nets last a week.

USES: To accent a seafood platter or to drape over a presentation of a whole fish. The nets look attractive when trailed off deck of a Daikon sailboat and, as described below, can be hung like a hammock between green pepper palm trees.

1. **Trim carrot section into a rectangular block, conserving as much of carrot's thickness as possible.** Edges of cuts can be rounded. Mix salt and water; soak carrot in brine at least 8 hours to soften, unrefrigerated.

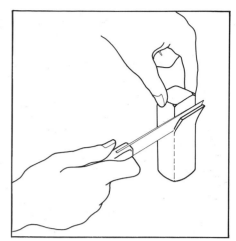

2. When carrot is pliable pass ice pick lengthwise through center of block. Replace ice pick with skewer.

3. To cut weave pattern make many parallel cuts rather close together and absolutely straight up and down as described below. If blade angles slightly to right or left you will cut holes in the net. It is also important to hold your blade straight out so its cutting edge is parallel to cutting board. At end of each cut lift blade straight up rather than slicing back out of cut. There is actually only 1 cut; straight down through top surface of block to skewer. Then knife is lifted up and out, carrot is turned so another surface is on top and cut is repeated. The weave is quite simple. **Number sides of block: 1 is top, 2 is right side, 3 is bottom and 4 is left side.** Begin 1/8 inch in from 1 end. Cut straight down to skewer. Turn block over so side 3 is on top. Cut down to skewer *directly over* first cut. If skewer hadn't stopped blade you would have just cut an 1/8-inch thick slice off end. Now turn carrot so side 2 is on top. Move down length of carrot another 1/8 inch and make cut to skewer. Lift blade out, turn block so side 4 is on top and cut down directly above cut you just made on side 2. That's it. Now you repeat pattern down length of carrot: 1:3 move, 2:4 move, 1:3 move, 2:4 move. **If you lose your place, just remember no full cut on any side is ever immediately followed by another full cut. Just look for 2 half cuts on a top side to begin again with a full cut.**

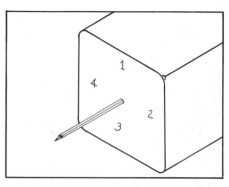

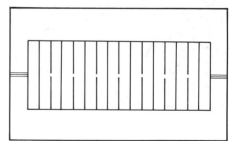

4. To peel carrot into a sheet you'll be cutting toward your hand. If this upsets your concentration, hold block with a cloth in your hand. **Leave skewer in carrot. Lay knife along side of carrot. Cut into carrot using a gentle but steady pressure and a short sawing motion. Rotate carrot into blade and pare off corners of block, shaping it into a cylinder.** Let corners fall away in pieces, they are not part of net. Now lay blade on length of this cylinder and cut under its surface no deeper than thickness of a nickel. Using same combination of rotating carrot into gently sawing blade, give carrot 3 or 4 gradual revolutions until you have peeled a sheet away and are cutting near skewer.

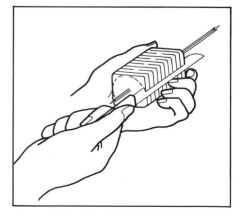

5. Set knife down; remove skewer. The net is done. If you want little round cork floats attached to end of your net, then complete cuts between remaining round sections of core. If cork floats don't interest you, simply slice core piece off. Handle net gently. If it doesn't stay open, peeling cut was too thick. Let stiff net rest on a dish, uncovered for a half a day and it will become much more flexible.

Daikon & Pineapple Palm Tree

INGREDIENTS: 1 large, bushy pineapple top, 1 long firm and fairly straight Daikon radish, 1 (3-inch-thick) watermelon end piece and a few green olives or kumquats.

TOOLS & SUPPLIES: Paring knife, 6-inch knife, vegetable peeler, scoring tool, an ice pick, 2 wood skewers and wooden picks.

TIPS & TIMING: The radish should be cold and hard. Select a pineapple whose top is quite full and well fanned out. If top is a bit sparse, pull a dozen extra leaves from other pineapples as you shop. Trim soft white bottoms from these extra leaves and insert them among leaves of finished palm to flesh it out. The design takes 15 minutes to create and keeps very well for 3 days. Wrap and refrigerate top separately.

USES: A table top accent for parties with a tropical theme.

1. If radish is fairly clean (free from hair and discolorations), you need not peel it. Cut off both ends. **Use scoring tool to cut inch long grooves into its surface.** These grooves are made at a right angle to length of radish.

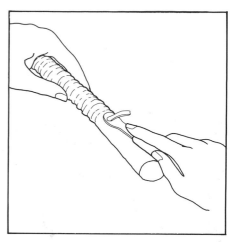

2. Set watermelon piece flat side down. Hold radish trunk on top of melon and trace outline of trunk's base into melon skin with tip of your knife. Put trunk aside and cut a hole down through melon. Push bottom of trunk clear through base. If hole is too narrow shave base of trunk with peeler, then fit narrowed trunk into it. If hole is too big, hold trunk in place and pass 2 or 3 skewers in through sides of base deep enough to penetrate trunk, then snip off exposed skewer ends with a pair of shears.

3. Twist leafy top off pineapple. Cut base of leaf stem flat. Poke 2 holes into core of leaf stem with ice pick. Cut skewers to 4 inch lengths. **Push blunt ends of skewers into holes, then stick skewered pineapple top onto trunk. For coconuts, attach a few green olives or kumquats to top of trunk with wooden pick points.**

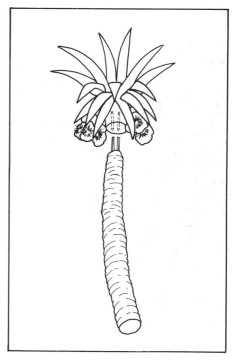

Green Pepper Palm Tree

INGREDIENTS: 1 firm, long carrot, 1 large green bell pepper, 1 large potato or a pineapple end cut.

TOOLS & SUPPLIES: Paring knife, vegetable peeler, wooden pick and a pitcher of cold water.

TIPS & TIMING: Cutting time is 10 minutes. The cut pepper should soak in cold water overnight. The tree keeps well 4 days. Use a cold carrot straight from the refrigerator.

USES: As a table accent for a luau or party with a seaside or tropical theme.

1. Insert your knife through topmost point of stem end of pepper. Cut completely around stem and remove it. Set pepper down with its open end facing up. **Cut out a series of deep V's whose tops intersect thus creating branches. These branches should be 2 to 3 inches long and 1-1/2 inches wide at top when turned upright. Cut 2 small notches out of each side of each branch. Make a single slice down through bottom of each major V.** Put pepper in cold water and soak it overnight in refrigerator. This will spread branches out.

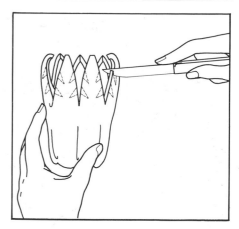

2. Trim ends off carrot and peel it. There are various ways to texture carrot into a palm tree trunk. One is to cut out short horizontal notches with a scoring tool. Another calls for cutting notches out with a paring knife. **The preferred way is to make shallow downward cuts just under surface. These are incomplete cuts; they remain attached at bottom and their tops are manually bent out.** They'll curl out even more when tree is displayed.

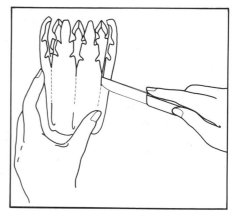

3. For base, cut potato (the economy island) in half along its length or use end cut from a pineapple, (the deluxe tropical island) at least 1 inch thick. Set bottom of carrot trunk in middle of base, score a line around it, then cut a hole for trunk going completely through base. Press trunk into base.

4. To display tree, push a wooden pick point into top of trunk leaving a quarter inch exposed. Set opened pepper onto tip of pick.

5. You can convert a carrot net into a hammock by threading a short skewer through weaving at both ends. First fold each end/over once, then thread skewer through double thickness. Of course, if your net's a bit on thick side, you can skip folding over step. Lash hammock between 2 carved palm trees, notching their trunks and securing skewers to trees with kitchen string. Cover string with wilted green onion leaves as pictured, if desired.

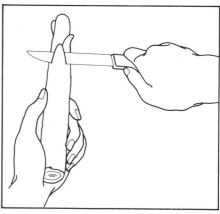

Pineapple Turtle

INGREDIENTS: 1 large, firm pineapple, 1 red radish and 1 ripe olive.

TOOLS & SUPPLIES: Paring knife and 1 (6-inch) wood skewer.

TIPS & TIMING: Carving time is 20 minutes. The turtle keeps for 3 days. If a leg breaks off just reattach it with a wooden pick. The head may droop after a day; simply reinsert it at a steeper angle.

USES: As a table decoration for tropical parties and parties to honor completion of a lengthy project. You can also give this as a nudge to someone whose lethargy has been driving you crazy!

1. Twist and pull leafy top off fruit. Save one leaf for tail.

2. **Refer to drawing. Cut and remove head/neck section first. The cut along neck should be at least 1/2 inch deep; head, 1 inch deep. Note, however, this is one continuous piece. To remove this section insert your knife at base of neck and undercut outline of head/neck section.**

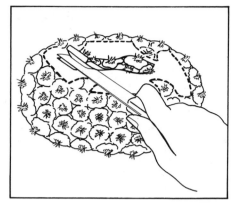

3. **Cut outline of feet and bottom of shell as drawn. Pare away all skin from around feet and shell bottom but wait to undercut and loosen feet until later.**

4. **The pattern of back shell is a 6-sided "plate" in center at top. It is surrounded by a row of smaller six-sided plates. The bottom of shell is simply broken into plates whose sides will vary in number depending on pineapple skin you have left to work with. Four-sided plates will do. Cut outline of plates by making opposing V cuts and lifting out 1/4 inch wide sections of skin from between cuts.**

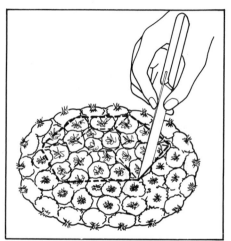

5. Now cut under feet 1/2 inch thick. Bend them out and set body on its feet; insert wooden picks in legs to stiffen them. Attach head by inserting a 6-inch skewer down through stem end of fruit at a 45 degree angle. Slip neck onto skewer.

6. Cut blunt end off pineapple leaf. The pointed tail should be 3 inches long. Cut a horizontal slit into back of body and insert blunt end of leaf into slit, curving down slightly.

7. For eyes, take 2 small slices off side of a red radish. Press flat side of slices against sides of head. The pineapple's moisture will effect a bond. Cut 2 tiny pieces of black olive skin and place one in center of each red radish eye.

Pineapple Spiral

INGREDIENTS: 1 large firm pineapple with a full leafy top.

TOOLS & SUPPLIES: Paring knife and a 6-inch knife.

TIPS & TIMING: Carving time is 10 minutes. The spiral keeps well for 4 days. Be sure tip of your paring knife is stiff and quite sharp.

USES: By itself spiral is an attractive centerpiece for fruit platters on all occasions. It is also a striking and efficient way to serve fruit skewers. Simply place a row of skewers into each groove like a large pincushion.

1. Cut 1/2 inch off bottom of fruit. Set it on its cut bottom near front of your cutting board.

2. Keep fruit upright as you work. Rolling pineapple on its sides will mash edges of spiral. You work near front of cutting board because your hand must necessarily be lower than fruit in order to cut bottom of each groove at correct angle. Cut top side of each groove while you are standing over pineapple and bottom side of each groove sitting or kneeling a little lower than fruit.

3. Insert a wooden pick a little ways into an eyelet at very top. The wooden pick helps to relocate top of first cut. The grooves of spiral are made by cutting out strips of skin that spiral down around sides following diagonal path of a row of eyelets. Each strip is as wide as a row of eyelets. The key to success here is in cutting shallow strips of skin and just a little flesh. Deep narrow grooves are unattractive and too weak to hold fruit skewers.

4. **Insert your knife just above wooden pick. Angle blade downward just under skin. Don't point it into center of fruit—that's too deep. With tip of blade 1/2 inch under surface, saw cut down along top of row of eyelets.** Near bottom make cut more shallow in order to retain a solid base. As you work, turn fruit into blade so you are always cutting into it in a natural, comfortable position. **Go back to top of row, insert tip of your knife under wooden pick, aiming up, and saw cut along bottom of row of eyelets.** Remember to make groove extra shallow at bottom.

5. Pull strip between cuts out of fruit. Start next cut 1/8 inch to right of this first groove. Leaving a thin bead of dark skin intact accentuates lines of spiral. (If you are left handed, work to left of groove you just made.)

6. Proceed, making shallow grooves parallel to first all around surface of fruit. It often happens that there is a portion of uncut skin left near bottom of fruit while top is already completely filled in with grooves. Simply fill in uncut space with shorter grooves.

Zucchini & Chili Parrot

INGREDIENTS: 1 thick zucchini slightly curved near stem and 7 inches long or longer; 3 chilies, all slightly curved; 1 small Serrano chili preferably turning from green to orange, 1 standard yellow chili and 1 long green chili; 2 green onions; 2 (1/8-inch) slices from neck of a butternut squash and 3 pineapple leaves.

TOOLS & SUPPLIES: Paring knife, 6-inch knife, 2 wood skewers and wooden picks.

TIPS & TIMING: Cutting and assembling parrot take 30 minutes. It keeps for 3 days. The wings may partially fall out during storage. Simply reattach them once you have placed parrot in its display position.

USES: Mount parrot on top or edge of watermelon birdcage or by itself on a squash that you have carved a few primitive designs into. This is a colorful addition to luaus and summer parties.

1. The body: **Slice off front lower section of zucchini starting halfway down its length under curve of stem. This cut passes from front to back, is slightly bowed and gives parrot a pale yellow belly.**

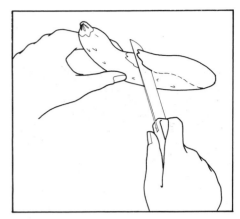

2. Beak: Cut stem off small Serrano chili. Hollow a groove out of top of zucchini stem the same width as chili. Push a half wooden pick into back of groove leaving it partially exposed. Fit cut end of chili into groove securing it on pick. The beak curves down.

3. Eyes: Make these from cross sections of base of chili stems or substitute slices of maraschino cherry or red radish. Attach eyes with wooden pick points.

4. Legs: Cut skewers to 5 inch lengths. **Make 2 Green Onion Brushes (page 25) and slip 1 onto middle of each skewer.** Push skewers up into top of stomach area of zucchini body. Flare top of onion brushes against body and mount body on a suitable base before going on.

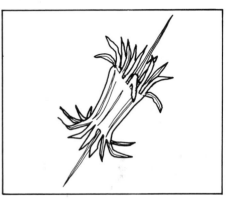

5. Wings: There are 3 wings on each side. All are attached with wooden pick points. The yellow chili is for bottom wings; squash slices for middle and long green chili is for large upper wing. **Cut 2 wings from each chili by slicing down alongside stem, through chili and out pointed tip.** Cut squash slices into shape of a comma, a crescent with a rounded top. Substitute carrot for squash if you wish.

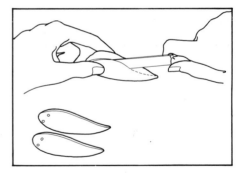

6. Attaching wings: Push 2 wooden pick points through skin side of top of yellow wings. Press points into body a few inches up from bottom. The yellow skin faces out. Attach orange wings above yellow in same way. Position wings so they cover wooden picks in lower wing. Pare top of green chili wings so they will fit snugly against body. Again, skin side of wings face out from body. Press blunt ends of 2 wooden pick points into flesh side of upper "shoulder" area of each green wing. Now push wings onto upper portion of body so these wings cover wooden picks in top of middle wings. If desired, extra chili strips can be attached to outer wings.

7. Tail: Cut white ends off pineapple leaves. Cut pointed leaves to 3 lengths—3 to 5 inches long. Trim their blunt ends to points. Cut 3 slits across lower back of body, one on top of another. Pass your paring knife up into body while making these slits. Insert cut end of longest leaf into lowest slit, middle-sized leaf into middle slit and smallest leaf into top slit.

Eggplant Penguin

INGREDIENTS: 1 medium to large eggplant with a rounded teardrop shape, 1 small carrot section and lemon juice.

TOOLS & SUPPLIES: Paring knife, wooden picks and a pastry brush.

TIPS & TIMING: Carving time is 10 minutes. The penguin keeps for 3 days. Be sure to brush lemon juice onto eggplant flesh as soon as you can after peeling. Store feet and bow tie separately or lemon juice will turn them pink.

USES: As a comical table decoration for holiday and skiing parties.

1. Cut a 1/2-inch-thick slice off end of eggplant, opposite stem. The stem end remains uncut—the stem cap being penguin's hat. Save slice for tail. Refer to drawing. **Use tip of paring knife to draw line of beak, chest and wings just skin deep.** Starting from 1 side of chest, slip your blade under edge of chest skin and proceed to cut away skin inside line in 1 piece. Use a smooth stroke so flesh underneath will also have a smooth surface. This process exposes white chest and stomach as well as defining wing tips.

2. Now cut under skin of beak leaving it attached at its top. Bend beak straight out and insert a wooden pick under it to hold it up.

3. Cut small eyelid flaps, as pictured. Pare 2 rounds out of carrot for eyes and attach these under eyelids with wooden pick points. Put a tiny piece of eggplant skin onto each eye for pupils.

4. Use some leftover skin to cut out a small bow tie. Attach it to chest by pressing 2 wooden pick points part way into body and then push tie onto exposed points.

5. If desired, fashion a small tail from bottom slice, shaping it like a blunt wedge, slightly rounded on its wide side. Slip a wooden pick into lower back, about 1 inch up from bottom and push narrow end of tail onto pick up against body.

6. Cut 2 long, floppy webbed feet out of leftover skin. These do not attach to penguin. Simply tuck them under front when you display it.

Eggplant Owl

INGREDIENTS: 1 large round or oval eggplant, 2 medium mushrooms (of equal size), 1 (2-inch) carrot section, 2 pineapple leaves and lemon juice.

TOOLS & SUPPLIES: Paring knife, 6-inch knife, pastry brush and wooden picks.

TIPS & TIMING: Cutting time is 10 minutes. Brush lemon juice immediately on all exposed eggplant flesh and owl will keep for 3 days. It's a good idea to buy a few extra mushrooms to be sure of getting a well matched set of eyes.

USES: A table decoration for Fall, Halloween and any scholastic event.

1. Rest eggplant on its side and cut entire stem area straight off. Save stem for feet.

2. Slice off stem and 1/3 of cap from each mushroom. Brush cut surface of remaining 2/3 of each cap with lemon juice. These are eyes. They are attached side by side 1/3 of way down from top of eggplant when it is standing on its cut side. Space them a bit less than an inch apart. Hollow out 2 cavities the size of the mushrooms in the eggplant for eye sockets. Push a wooden pick into each cavity leaving their tips exposed. Push round side of eyes into cavities and onto wooden picks.

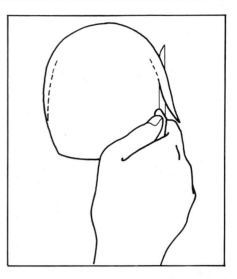

3. Beak: Pare carrot into shape of a short pointed bullet. Cut 1 side of it flat and stick it onto eggplant between eyes with a wooden pick point. Note that beak points down not out.

4. Wings: Use 6-inch knife to cut wings. Each wing is a simple flap cut up right and left side. **Start each flap an inch from bottom and cut up to shoulder area just above height of tops of eyes. If you wish, cut small notches out of edges of wings.** Manually bend them out from body a short ways. For a livelier looking owl, brace wings out from body using a wooden pick on each side under "wingpits".

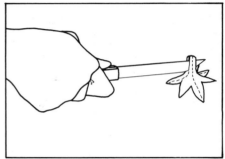

5. Feathers: Make feathers in front of body by cutting downward pointing V's into skin. Bend little V's up a bit.

6. Ears: Cut pineapple leaves down to 3 inch lengths. Cut a V-shaped slit into top of head above each eye. Push cut leaves into slits, points up.

7. Feet: Cut stem section into quarters. (For a sillier looking owl— one with overgrown feet, just cut stem section in half) Each quarter should be composed of stem, green stem cap leaf and a little eggplant. Select a pair of quarter sections for 2 feet. Choose 2 with plenty of green leaf cap. Trim away purple eggplant from edges of leaf caps. Cut notches out of bottom edge of leaf cap to give illusion of owls claws. Shave back corner of stems smooth. Press a wooden pick half into back of each foot and tack feet to base of owl.

Seasonal Designs

Having a party for the holidays or need a centerpiece for the table? Choose among these theme designs for Halloween, Thanksgiving, Christmas or Easter. Each can be made within 30 minutes and prepared up to 3 days in advance.

Ghosts & Goblins

INGREDIENTS: Cabbage ghost: 1/2 head of red cabbage, 2 cloves. Green goblin: 1 large, square-shaped green bell pepper, 2 small red chilies and 2 carrot slices. Whirling beastie: 1 small pineapple top and 2 small radishes.

TOOLS & SUPPLIES: Paring knife, 6-inch knife, pastry brush and wooden picks.

TIPS & TIMING: Shop for a cabbage head half whose core and main branches resemble a ghost with its arms extended upward. Bell pepper should have a flat bottom so that when cut in half, each half will still stand upright. Choose a pineapple top with a tight cluster of short leaves and center leaves that are strong and stick straight out. Each design takes but a few minutes to make and lasts up to 3 days.

USES: Platter and table decorations at a Halloween party. These designs are small and inexpensive. Display them near each other for a stronger effect.

1. Red Cabbage Ghost: Cut a full slice at least 1/2 inch thick off flat side of half cabbage. **Pare away smaller and outer leaves from this slice. Don't cut away leaves that immediately surround top of core; these form head of ghost. Pare away all main leaf stems except 2 arms.** With a wooden pick poke 2 eye holes into top of main core and hollow out an oval hole for mouth. Either fill 2 eye holes with cloves or leave them empty. Mount ghost on a wooden pick sticking out of remainder of cabbage half.

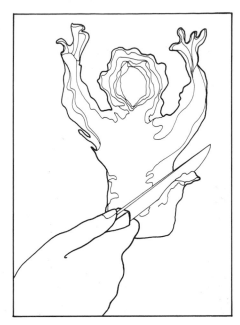

2. Green Bell Pepper Goblin: **Slice down through center of stem cutting pepper in half, positioning blade so it also passes through 2 opposite vertical indentations in outside walls of pepper.** Cut round carrot slices for eyes. Tuck 1 eye into each side of split seed pod. Insert wooden pick points in stem ends of chilies. Push points into top of bell pepper as shown in photo. That's all.

3. Whirling Beastie: Look into top of pineapple leaves. Decide which of interior straight leaves are suitable to represent a long pointed beak. Leave them in place and pluck next few rows of leaves out from around beak. Cut stem ends off 2 tiny red radishes giving these eyes small white centers. Push eyes into middle of plucked pineapple top, 1 on either side of beak.

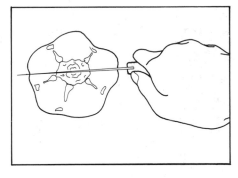

HALLOWEEN PUMPKINS

A sharp paring knife with a stiff blade is the best tool for carving pumpkins. Cut and remove the cap, then scoop out the seeds with a spoon in the standard fashion. It's smart to first draw your jack-o'-lantern face onto the pumpkin with a dry-erase, felt tipped marker before the actual face cutting begins. As you cut, angle the blade so the holes you are making will not narrow too much as they get deeper; this allows more light from the candle to shine out. Burn the short votive candles. Their flame isn't as likely to cook the top of the pumpkin as a tall candle, nor do they fall over while burning.

If you want to carve something other than the traditional face, look through the newspapers for store adds containing drawings of witches, bats and black cats. Cut the drawing out, tape it to the pumpkin, trace its silhouette onto the surface with a marker and cut it out. If you are displaying your carved pumpkin in front of a wall then cut a design into the back of the squash as well. The candle light will shine through the back and onto the wall. A bat shape or the word BOO *written backwards* are effective for this treatment.

Afternoon Halloween parties for children present the problem of too much daylight for the candle light to show up well. The solution is to decorate the outside of the pumpkin. Be sure to involve the children in the creation of their own designs. Use wooden picks to attach eyes, ears, noses, hair etc. An adult should assist the youngsters because it may be necessary to poke holes into the squash with an ice pick in order for the wooden picks to penetrate the tough pumpkin skin. For hair use cornsilk, cauliflower or moistened corn husks (fresh or dry). Noses can be fashioned from plum tomatoes, grapes, dried or fresh figs, chilies and olives, carrots, radishes and prunes. For eyes use radishes, stuffed olives, sliced mushroom rounds, grapes and kiwifruit slices. Wedges of long radishes, apples and plum tomatoes make lips and the tips of pineapple leaves can be used for fangs and sharp teeth. Hairy moles are made with green onion roots and, of course, you can draw scars, warpaint and tattoos on with felt tipped markers.

Don't overlook the wide variety of other squash also available for carving. For instance, cut a long face into an upright banana squash, then crown it with a Turban squash. Some stores now carry white pumpkins and blue skinned squash. There is also a variety called Golden Nugget which looks just like a miniature pumpkin that can be carved into a cute centerpiece for a Halloween party platter.

Pumpkins can be carved in intricate designs or combined with other vegetables to make faces. Directions for carving the pumpkin turkey is on page 128.

Napa Cabbage Angel

INGREDIENTS: 1 large head of cauliflower, 1 rather oval-shaped head of Napa cabbage at least 10 inches long, a 2-inch-wide turnip, 1 round slice of lemon or crooked neck squash, 2 cloves and 1 red radish.

TOOLS & SUPPLIES: Paring knife, 6-inch knife, vegetable peeler, 3 (10-inch) wood skewers and wooden picks.

TIPS & TIMING: Cutting and assembly takes 20 to 25 minutes. It keeps for 3 days. Store it without cloves in place; they stain the turnip. The wings and halo droop after a few hours on display. Have extra wings on hand. You may want to buy an extra cabbage for a wing supply. Store angel with its wings unattached, laid flush on body, wrapped in plastic.

USES: As a centerpiece for Christmas and Easter parties.

1. Cut bottom of cauliflower flat, eliminating all green leaves.

2. Carefully remove outer leaves from cabbage. Break them off from their bottoms, keeping leaves whole. Do this until you have a matched pair, suitable for angel wings. Trim bottom of cabbage (where leaves were attached) smooth.

3. The cabbage angel body stands on cauliflower "cloud" by means of 3 skewers. **Set cauliflower on its cut side and push skewers all way down through it to cutting board, tightly grouping skewers in center of cauliflower.** Hold cabbage upright next to skewers. If skewers are as high or higher than top of cabbage, remove skewers and cut them so they will be a few inches shorter than combined height of cauliflower and cabbage. Replace skewers, if necessary and slip cabbage straight down onto skewers—the leafy end points down.

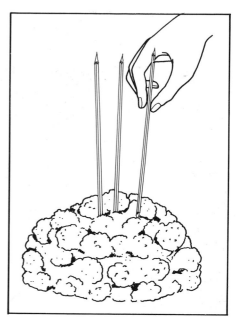

4. Head: Cut stem end off turnip, then peel it. If this yields a rather knobby noggin, use a bit of sandpaper to rub it smooth. Insert 2 cloves for eyes. Use tip of vegetable peeler to hollow out a little mouth. Cut a small tongue off side of red radish and place it in mouth.

5. Halo: Hollow out lemon or squash slice leaving its rim at least 1/4 inch thick. **Attach halo in an upright position at back of head by passing 2 wooden pick points through bottom of its rim into turnip.**

6. Hair: Use vegetable peeler to add hair to presently bald angel. Cut 1/2-inch-long upward slices in head at hairline in front and along sides. These cuts are incomplete; that is, you are not cutting anything off. When finished cutting, bend each cut up into a curl. Now attach head by inserting 2 wooden picks into bottom of head and sticking it onto top of cabbage body.

7. Wings: First lay 2 leaves side by side, curls down. Cut base off 1 on a diagonal going down to left, other down to right. The 1 on right will be right wing and the left leaf, the left wing. Pass 2 wooden picks halfway into thick rib at bottom of each leaf. Space picks at least 1/2 inch apart and have them parallel. One at a time, push each wing into shoulder blade area of angel body, holding bottom of each leaf by its rib.

Skiing Elf

INGREDIENTS: 1 zucchini 1 inch thick and 5 inches long (or longer), 2 bananas, 1 firm kiwifruit, 2 green onions with well-rounded white ends, 1 small turnip (or large pearl onion), 2 cloves, 1 Pasillo chili (or small green bell pepper), 1 cauliflower head, powdered sugar and lemon juice.

TOOLS & SUPPLIES: Paring knife, 6-inch knife, 4 (10-inch) wood skewers, wooden picks and a little boiling water.

TIPS & TIMING: This takes about 30 minutes to finish. It is same design idea as Gondolier on page Be sure to buy a chili that will fit onto turnip like a hat. The banana skins brown on their fleshy side; brush them with lemon juice to retard this. The elf keeps for 3 days. The banana skins need replacing after 1 day.

USES: As a table decoration for skiing and holiday parties.

1. Belt, scarf and leggings: Wilt green onion leaves in boiling water for 10 seconds. Cool and set these aside.

2. Eyes, nose and mouth: **Use a ridge off zucchini stem for nose.** Cloves are eyes although a nice substitute here are 2 crosswise slices from root end of a few very small red radish; they look more like skiing goggles. For a mouth, cut a tiny wedge out of a tiny radish. Now cut a second wedge just under first.

3. Legs: **Cut both ends off the zucchini, shortening it to 4 inches. Partially split it by cutting 3/4 of the way from top to bottom through center. Spread the legs slightly. Pass a wood skewer up through each leg until they come out the top about 1 inch.**

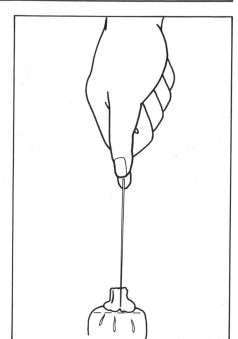

4. Torso: Cut the ends off the kiwifruit so the bottom matches the top of the zucchini and the top matches the bottom of the turnip head. Press the kiwifruit torso onto top of the zucchini legs.

5. Torso: Cut the ends off the kiwifruit so the bottom matches the top of the zucchini and the top matches the bottom of the turnip head. Press the kiwifruit torso onto top of the zucchini legs.

6. Pare the turnip down to a proper size or use a large pearl onion. Cut 1 end so it will rest flat on top of the kiwifruit torso. Before attaching the head, attach the eyes, nose, mouth and hair. Decide which wedge you want for a mouth and cut a wedged cavity out of turnip that will accommodate your desired mouth. Use green onion roots for hair. Use wooden pick points to attach them at an angle that makes hair windblown and swept back. Push a miniscule wooden pick point into cavity in turnip and push mouth onto it. Attach decorated head with a wooden pick.

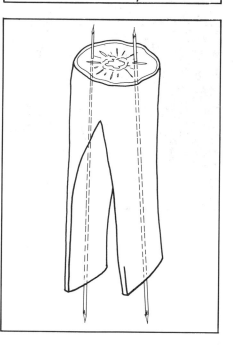

7. Arms: Use onions from making hair. Cut the white ends into 2 inch lengths. Slice a corner off the white ends to fit the shape of the kiwifruit at the "shoulders." Cut out a V-shaped wedge 1 inch from trimmed corner so arms will bend. Pass a 10-inch skewer through straight end of each onion for ski poles. Attach arms to body with wooden pick points.

8. To mount elf on skis, first cut off bottom of cauliflower, eliminating all green leaves; this is a snowy hilltop. For skis, cut all along inside curve of bananas including a little of stems. Trim stem ends to points. Lay skis skin side up on cauliflower and poke exposed bottoms of skewers through middle of skis and into cauliflower. Stabilize design by passing 2 wood skewer ski poles through each green onion hand and into cauliflower. If skis droop prop them up with wooden picks set under and parallel to ends of banana.

9. Push a wooden pick slightly into top of head. Hollow out chili from its stem end. Put chili hat on head, letting it rest against wooden pick. To display, dust elf with powdered sugar for snow.

Turnip Snowman

INGREDIENTS: 3 round turnips; small, medium and large, 1 bunch of red Swiss chard, 3 cranberries, 1 (1-inch) carrot section, 1 Pasillo chili (or small green bell pepper) or 1 tangelo with a raised stem end, 1 green onion (if desired) and cloves.

TOOLS & SUPPLIES: Vegetable peeler, paring knife, wooden picks and boiling water.

TIPS & TIMING: Cutting and assembly time is 15 minutes. The snowman keeps for 5 days but arms wilt after being on display 4 hours. Make extra arms for additional display periods. The chili is for the hat; its stem end should be wide enough to fit onto top of small turnip (the head).

USES: A table decoration for skiing and Winter holiday parties.

1. Peel turnips, trying to get 1 continuous strip from purple end of one. This peeling can be used as a scarf, if desired.

2. **Cut ends of turnips flat so they will fit flat and flush on top of each other when stacked—large, medium and small from bottom up. Use 2 wooden picks between each 2 turnips to stick them together.**

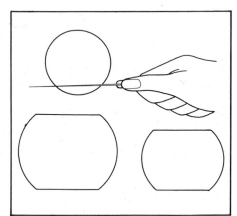

3. Cut cranberries in half crosswise. Push 5 or 6 wooden pick points, in a vertical row, into front of 2 lower turnips. Press flat sides of berries onto points for buttons.

4. Use cloves for eyes and also insert a smiling row of them for a mouth. (The cloves can stain turnip; remove them during storage.) Whittle carrot into a tiny carrot stick nose and attach it with a wooden pick point.

5. Hollow out chili (or pepper). Push a wooden pick a short ways into top of head, then set chili hat (perfect for chilly weather) over pick onto head. To match photo, cut stem end from tangelo; use for hat instead of chili.

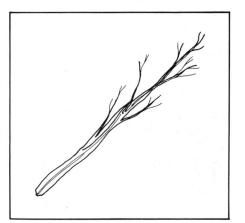

6. If desired, wilt green onion leaves in boiling water; use for a hatband, belt or scarf. Also try out purple strip from step 1, then use scarf you like best. To match photo, cut a long strip from remaining piece of tangelo with a zitrus scorer.

7. **The arms are stems of red Swiss chard leaves. Pare away green leafy matter. Try to include a few side branches of stem veins on your arms as well. The bottom of each arm should be 1/4 inch wide.** Mount arms on wooden pick points stuck into each shoulder at upward angles. Make an extra set of arms for every additional time you intend to display snowman. Store all arms separately in a damp paper towel wrapped in plastic. Attach arms just before you display this design.

Randolf, the Red-Nosed Rainmoose

INGREDIENTS: 1 large Bosc pear, 2 ginger roots, 1 cranberry or maraschino cherry, bottom ends of 2 crooked neck squash (or lemons) and 1 radish.

TOOLS & SUPPLIES: Paring knife and wooden picks.

TIPS & TIMING: Carving time is 5 minutes. It keeps well for 3 days. When buying ginger root, look for 2 pieces that resemble a pair of antlers.

USES: As a comical platter decoration at Christmas time.

1. Cut stem off pear. **Cut a slice off 1 side of round end of pear so it can rest on this cut with its narrow end slightly elevated.**

2. **Trim bottoms of ginger roots so they will fit flush on top of pear's round end. Push 2 wooden picks halfway into bottom of each root.** Stick ginger root antlers into pear, as pictured.

3. The squash (or lemon) ends are eyes. Cut 2 thin slices from radish. Use wooden pick points to attach radish slices to pear just in front of antlers leaving ends exposed. Push squash ends onto pick points.

4. Trim 1 side off cranberry or cherry. Push a wooden pick half into stem end of pear leaving its tip exposed, then press flat side of cranberry nose onto pick.

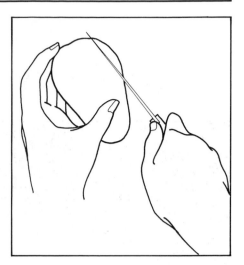

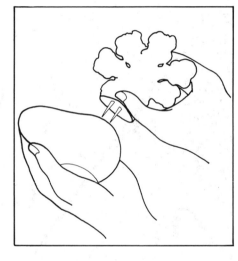

Daikon Candle

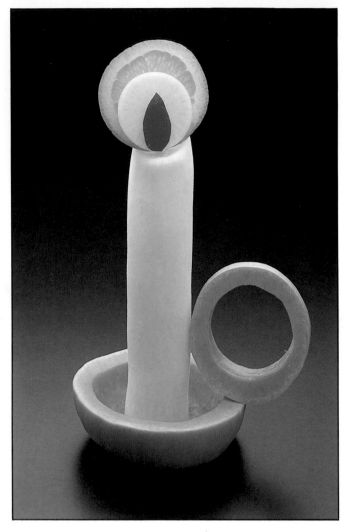

INGREDIENTS: 1 fairly large butternut squash, 1 (10-inch) straight daikon radish, 1 small orange and 1 red radish.

TOOLS & SUPPLIES: Paring knife, 6- and 9-inch knives, a spoon, 3 (4-inch) wood skewers and 3 wooden picks.

TIPS & TIMING: Carving time is 15 minutes. The candle keeps for 3 days but flame components may need replacing after each display.

USES: As a Winter holiday table decoration.

1. Base and handle: With large knife cut a 1-1/2-inch-thick slice off bottom of squash. **Etch a line into cut side 1 inch in from edge all around.** Scoop cut a smooth depression 1/2 inch deep within this circular line. Cut a 1/2-inch-thick round slice from neck of squash. Hollow it out so rim is 1/2 inch wide.

2. Candle: Peel daikon radish. Slice both ends flat. Cut 2 (1/4-inch-thick) slices from 1 end and set these aside. The radish should have an even thickness along its length. Use vegetable peeler to even it out, if necessary. Trim 1 end to look like top of a burning candle by cutting across it at a slight angle then, hollow out top of cut a bit.

3. Attach candle to stand by pushing 3 skewers, points up, straight down into depression in wide squash slice. Push radish candle onto skewers and push it tightly into base. Set small squash slice straight up on edge of base and attach it with 2 wooden pick points, 1 into base, the other into candle.

4. Flame: **Slice side off red radish. Trim slice to an oval with a curving point. Attach it, point up and red side out, to 1 of round daikon slices using a wooden pick point. Cut a fairly thick crosswise slice from orange. Stick daikon radish slice to orange slice.** Use a wooden pick point going through base of flame and into pithy bottom of orange slice to effect bond. Have flame burning up from edge of orange slice and in front of its center. Attach this flame to top of candle by pushing a half wooden pick, point up, partially into top of daikon candlesticks, then setting bottom of orange slice onto pick.

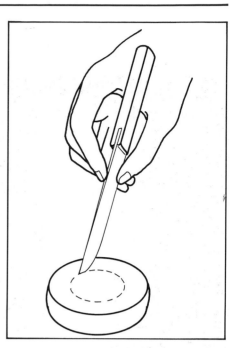

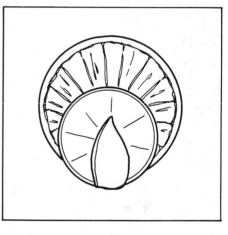

Cabbage Christmas Tree

INGREDIENTS: 1 large green cabbage, about 10 green onion leaves, 1 carrot section, 6 cranberries or other bits of colorful food cut into circles and diamonds.

TOOLS & SUPPLIES: 6-inch knife, a small star-shaped cookie or aspic cutter, a little boiling water and wooden picks.

TIPS & TIMING: Cutting tree takes 2 minutes; decorating takes 10 minutes. Be sure cabbage is large. The leaves of small cabbages are too densely packed to create right illusion. The tree lasts 5 days and can then be shaved and used for another 3 days. The decorations usually need replacing every 3 days.

USES: A table decoration for Christmas parties.

1. Conserving as much leafy material as possible, cut bottom of cabbage flat. Stand it on its flat bottom. **Hold 1 fingertip on very top of cabbage, then slice entire head into shape of an upside down cone, shaving down along its sides using 10 or 12 strokes with 6-inch knife, turning cabbage slightly between each stroke.** The top of the cabbabe will fall away unless you hold it in place.

2. Push a wooden pick down through top of tree leaving its tip exposed. Cut a star from a carrot slice using aspic cutter, and place it on pick.

3. To decorate tree, first wilt green onions in boiling water for 10 seconds. **Place rows of wooden pick halves around tree, their points left exposed. Drape green onions on tree attaching their ends to points of picks. Cap each pick with a half cranberry or other small bits of colorful food.** Arrange small vegetable presents around base of tree, if desired.

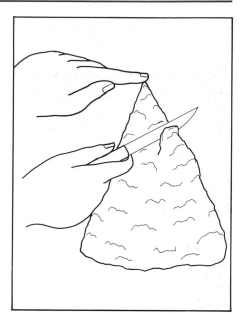

Pineapple Christmas Tree

INGREDIENTS: 1 pineapple with a fresh very full set of leaves, 1 red apple, powdered sugar and cranberries or raspberries, if desired.

TOOLS & SUPPLIES: Paring knife, 6-inch knife, 2 (6-inch) skewers and a star-shaped cookie or aspic cutter.

TIPS & TIMING: Cutting time is 10 minutes. The tree keeps for 5 days. When buying pineapple, turn it upside down. The key to this design is selecting a pineapple whose upside down top definitely looks like a Christmas tree.

USES: A table decoration at Christmas parties.

1. **Cut pineapple crosswise 3 inches from leafy top.** Cut 2 side pieces off remaining fruit, leaving a 1/2-inch-thick slice in middle attached to core of leaves.

2. Use star cutter to mark shape of star into 1 side of middle of attached slice just above leaves. The cutter will not pass through pineapple. **Cut fruit away from star shape with a paring knife, leaving pineapple star attached to base of leaves.**

3. Use apple as a base on which to stand tree. Cut a slice off wider end of apple and set it on this cut side. Stick 2 skewers straight down through apple and slip tree, star side up, onto skewers. Dust tree with powdered sugar. You may also want to string cranberries with a needle and thread, and wind garland of cranberries around tree.

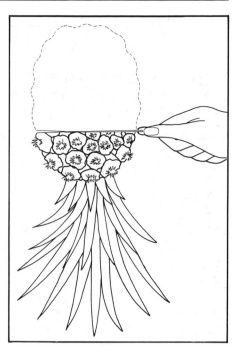

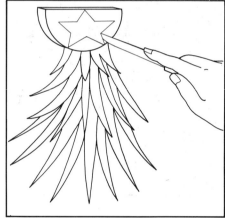

Apple Turkey

INGREDIENTS: A large, unbruised Red Delicious apple and a saucer of lemon juice.

TOOLS & SUPPLIES: Paring knife, 6-inch knife, wooden picks and turkey head pattern (page 140).

TIPS & TIMING: Carving time is 20 minutes. It keeps for 3 days. As you work, immediately dip each cut surface in lemon juice. Store turkey with small tips of tail feathers unextended. Be sure tip of your paring knife is straight and sharp. This design has about 9 jillion cuts to make, although most are very simple. Take heart and just start; you'll be done before you know it. By the way, virtually ALL of apple is used so do refrain from snacking on it lest you inadvertently devour a wing or tail feather (which happens all too often when I teach this design just before lunch!).

USES: As a platter decoration for Thanksgiving and Christmas parties.

1. Remove stem. Cut off wide end of apple in 1 smooth slice, cutting into stem depression (slice should be about 1/2 inch thick). Set this slice aside; it will become the tail.

2. Rest apple on its cut end. Place 6-inch knife across 2 bumps on top; cut down through apple, making slice for head and side wings.

3. Head: **Lay turkey head pattern on flat side of slice from step 2. Cut straight across slice just in front of beak. Trace pattern into apple section.** Wipe pattern dry and put it away. Block cut around traced head and neck. Hold your paring knife at a right angle to flat side of apple section, cut out form using a gentle pressure and steady short sawing strokes.

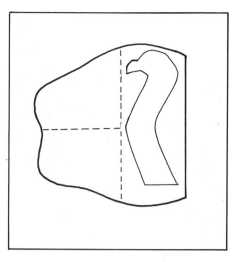

4. Wattle: Hold head with skin facing you. Trim a thin strip of skin from lower back of neck, continuing up over top of head and stop cutting only when you reach middle of top of beak; leave attached at beak. Pare fleshy side of beak to a point. Trim fleshy side of neck, smoothing edges. Fold strip over top of beak; lay head, flesh side down, so wattle is held under it. If wattle breaks off, cut a slit across top of beak; tuck 1 end of wattle into slit.

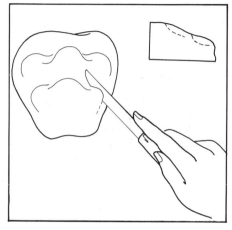

5. Side wings: **Lay remainder of slice from step 2 flat-side down. Put your knife between 2 bumps and cut slice in half.** The 2 cut sides of each of 2 half pieces you just made are left as is. Cut thin V-shaped wedges out of curved sides of these pieces where skin is touching cutting board. Remove wedges. Turn side wings over and pare away some of flesh under wing tips.

6. Body: **Feather body in 2 steps. (A) Hold your paring knife near top of back of apple, its cutting edge facing to front (the narrow end). One-half inch in from back edge of top, cut under skin at a very shallow angle. Cut forward 1/2 inch, then dip angle of your blade deeper into apple and cut forward another 1/2 inch. Remove knife. Do this again starting just forward of end of preceeding cut. Repeat these 2 cuts on upper portion of both sides of apple. In all, there are 6 cuts to this step. (B) Make skin deep slashes into each of loosened flaps of skin made in step A. The direction of these slashes is oriented toward center of front of body.** In effect, step A made a cut something like a fan. Step B cuts ribs into edges of each fan. With edge of your blade, bend tips of fans (feathers) up slightly. Pour a little lemon juice into these cuts.

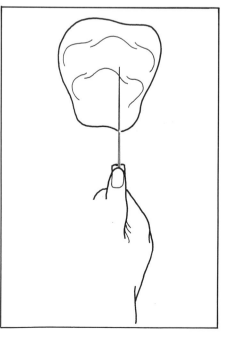

7. Tail: Hold round slice from step 1 against rear of apple. Elevate it so stem hole is 1/2 inch above top edge of body and have skin facing forward. The thick part of slice should be level with top of body. Poke a dotted line into skin of slice, following contour of back of body. Lay slice down and cut along dotted line. Position larger piece to see if it fits onto top of back edge of body. It needn't be perfect; bottom edges may stick out a little.

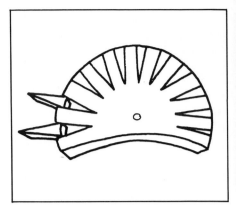

8. Tail feathers: Lay tail piece flat side down. Using hole in its interior as a target, cut wedges into slice all around its curved perimeter. Now, this is very important; these wedges should be a good 1/2 inch long and nearly 1/4 inch wide at outer edge where skin touches cutting board. And this is even more critical: wedges do not touch each other along outside edge. There must be a rib between each wedge and these ribs should be at least 1/8 inch thick. As you cut, leave wedges in place. Do not remove them.

9. Assembly: Cut a small cavity out of top of body at its extreme front into which bottom of neck will fit. Push a wooden pick halfway into this cavity and slip neck down pick and into cavity. Attach each side wing with 2 wooden pick halves. Position wings so 1 fleshy side faces front and wooden picks pass through other fleshy side which is against body. To attach tail, press 2 whole wooden picks straight down into body 1/4 inch in from back edge just right and left of center. Push tail piece onto picks, seating it down on back of body. When you are ready to display turkey you then extend tail feathers made in step 7. One by one, lift each wedge out of its slot and fit it backwards back into same slot, blunt edge first. Force corners on skin side of each wedge into flesh of ribs so tips of feathers will stay put. Do so with red skin facing forward—or to rear whichever appeals to you more.

PUMPKIN TURKEY (photo on page 111)

1. To make a pumpkin turkey, use a 6- to 8-inch pumpkin. Use the head pattern on page 141. If pumpkin is larger, use head pattern as a guide and enlarge it in proportion to the size of pumpkin. Steps for making pumpkin turkey are the same as for the apple turkey except for steps below. Lemon juice is not necessary to prevent browning.

2. Cut out and remove pumpkin stem. Don't cut a hole in front of pumpkin for the head to fit into. Instead carve bottom of neck so it rests snugly on natural curve of top front of pumpkin.

3. Feathers: Using a zester, cut into the skin, pulling the zester toward the front of the turkey. Cut 1/2-inch-long strips, then pull zester backwards, leaving strips attached to pumpkin.

4. Use an ice pick or skewer to poke holes in the pumpkin to attach the tail, wings and head. Wooden picks may break during attaching unless the holes are already pierced.

Butter

There are a number of ways to enliven the presentation of butter, all of which are simple and can be prepared days and even weeks ahead.

To shape individual butter portions into stars, hearts and scallops, fill a pastry bag fitted with a star or scallop tip with softened butter (or margarine). Pipe the shapes onto a cutting board covered with wax paper. Wrap the paper around the bottom of the board so it doesn't slip or lift off the board as you pipe the butter onto it. Set the board into the freezer for 30 minutes. Remove it and peel the paper away from the individual shapes. For temporary storage, place the shapes into ice water. For longer storage, place shapes in a plastic freezer bag and freeze them. To serve, place frozen butters on a serving dish; thaw in the refrigerator before serving.

To serve a steak, fish fillet, vegetable or starch with the butter shape already on it, apply the butter about 30 seconds before serving so the shape is recognizeable yet just beginning to melt.

Butter curls are another attractive mode of presenting butter or margarine. These are made with a special tool, a knife whose blade is curled into a hook shape and is slightly corrugated. First heat the blade in very hot water. The butter should stand out of the refrigerator 20 minutes before any curls are attempted. Very cold butter simply cracks and very warm butter is too soft to hold a curled shape. Margarine can be worked immediately; no waiting is necessary. Hold the blade at a right angle to the surface of the butter cube and pull smoothly across its top. Tap each curl into a bowl of very cold water. Later, handle chilled curls with a fork or slotted spoon; even a little heat from your fingers will begin to melt them out of shape.

Butter balls are formed with a warmed melon baller, however, the balls seldom come out perfectly round. To perfect their shape, tap the balls into cold water for a moment, then use a pair of wood butter paddles to rub them into a better form. Hold paddles with their handles at a right angle to each other and rub the butter ball between their flat surfaces.

Wood, ceramic and metal molds can be rather frustrating due to their tendency to cling to the butter. Plastic and rubber molds release the butter shapes more readily. To properly coat the mold use a soft brush or your fingertips to paint very soft butter onto its surface, eliminating all air bubbles. Then fill the mold to its top and scrape it smooth. Let the molded butter harden in the freezer. To unmold turn the mold upside down and bend it slightly letting the butter fall into a cold water bath.

Use aspic cutters or vegetable punches for yet another way to create novel presentations. First spread softened butter onto a cutting board covered with wax paper. Chill the butter, then cut it with a variety of warmed cutters. The cut shapes will tend to stick to the paper. Leave them on the paper, rechill them, then peel the paper off the individual pieces.

All these techniques work equally well with flavored butters such as Maitre'd, a compound of butter, lemon and parsley. Professional cooks often make up a large volume of a compound butter recipe, then spoon or pipe thick lines of it onto sheets of parchment paper. The paper is rolled into a tube around the butter, chilled and later cut into round slices and served on an appropriate hot food.

Try these flavored butter recipes. Each begins with 1/4 pound of lightly salted butter.

Maitre'd: Add 1 tablespoon fresh lemon juice, 2 tablespoons finely chopped parsley and a pinch of white pepper. Use on steaks, fish and green vegetables.

Ligurian: Add 2 tablespoons minced

sun-dried tomatoes in olive oil, 1 tablespoon chopped fresh basil and a pinch of garlic powder. Use on chicken, veal, pork and pasta.

Chaps: To the Maitre'd recipe, add 1 teaspoon each minced, sautéed garlic and shallot, 1 tablespoon chopped fresh tarragon, 2 tablespoons concentrated beef stock (or demi-glace) and a dash of brandy. Use this on broiled red meats.

Chocolate

CHOCOLATE ACCENTS

A list of ingredients for pure chocolate would quite simply read: Cocoa and cocoa butter. Because so simple a chocolate bar would be rather bitter, sugar and vanilla are often added to sweeten and mellow it. Lecithin, an emulsifier, is another common additive; it helps to keep the cocoa butter from separating out of the mixture. Cocoa butter is simply the natural oil extracted from the cocoa beans during the manufacture of cocoa powder. It melts below body temperature and gives real chocolate its deliciously quick melting quality. Of course, it's also the cocoa butter that gives chocolate its reputation for being tricky to work with. Some manufacturers (and cooks) try to get around the problem of the cocoa butter separating out and rising to the surface as a grey *bloom* by using a cocoa butter substitute like palm kernel oil and even paraffin; but they ruin the lovely melting quality just mentioned.

Whether you are working with dark, milk or white chocolates you can control and stabilize the cocoa butter in them by a careful melting process called *tempering*. Briefly, properly tempered chocolate is melted to 110F (45C), cooled to 81F (25C), then rewarmed to 86-89F (30C). The chocolate is still liquid and is used for dipping, painting and drawing.

The tempering process takes about 20 minutes. You'll need a low temperature thermometer (there are special chocolate thermometers, but a yogurt thermometer also works and is more commonly available), a rubber spatula, a metal spatula and a pastry scraper, a thin metal mixing bowl, a pan into which the bowl will partially fit and a smooth, cool surface (marble slab, Formica counter or stainless steel table top).

TEMPERING:

1. Chop the chocolate into pea-sized bits by hand. A food processor can overheat it.

2. Bring 2 inches of water to a boil in the pan. Turn the heat off and let the water cool a few degrees. Put the chocolate bits in the bowl; set it over, not in, the water. Immediately begin to stir it around, always scraping across the bottom of the bowl with the rubber spatula. When it is lukewarm 110F (45C), remove bowl from heat. Wipe bottom of the bowl dry, and pour the warm chocolate into a second bowl. Or simply dip the bottom of the bowl in cool water for a few seconds, then wipe it dry. Never let water touch melted chocolate. The chocolate will seize up into a doughy clay. If you heat chocolate beyond 120F (49C), you have ruined it. Overheated chocolate will be grainy in texture, and its surface will be streaked with grey rivers of hardened cocoa butter.

3. Pour half the melted chocolate onto a cool, smooth surface. If you use a marble board, don't chill it in the refrigerator. The cool surface should be around 65F (18C). If it is too cold, the chocolate hardens too fast. Use the metal spatula to scrape the chocolate around until it cools, begins to thicken to a thin toothpaste consistency and is taking on a slightly dull sheen. Scrape this cooled chocolate back into

For a more interesting presentation, butter can be piped with a pastry bag, pressed into plastic molds or rolled in balls.

the bowl of warm chocolate, and stir them together.

4. The chocolate should feel cool but probably needs further stirring to get down to 81F (27C). At that temperature it will feel surprisingly cold for something that looks so warm and luscious.

5. Bring the chocolate back up to 86F (30C). This takes just a few seconds over the hot water. The safe range to work in is 86-89F (30C). If you ever heat it up to 93F (34C) or hotter, you will have to start the whole process over. Beyond 92F (33C) the cocoa butter becomes released again and will cause streaking. As you proceed to make chocolate accents, you'll be putting the bowl of chocolate back on the hot water to keep it from cooling too much. Never leave it there unstirred and never leave it there for more than 10 to 15 seconds at a time—it reheats very fast!

At this point you have a very stable chocolate suitable for all of the following chocolate accents. After doing it a few times you'll find the process simple and rewarding. Set aside a full morning to create lots of accents for months to come. It's best to do this when the room temperature is close to 65F (18C). Although brief periods of refrigeration are called for during the making of chocolate leaves, cups and shells, do not store chocolate in the refrigerator or the freezer. Moisture will condense on its surface and cause crystallization. Keep all chocolates in a cool cupboard—55F (13C) is the optimum storage temperature. Plain dark chocolate contains a natural anti-oxidant and can last up to ten years! Milk and white chocolate contain milk solids that can spoil after eight months.

CHOCOLATE CURLS

With a metal spatula, spread a smooth layer of tempered chocolate as thick as a nickel, and up to six inches wide, across the marble or counter top. Let it firm up stiff but not brittle. Hold a sharp chef's knife at a 45 degree angle to the layer and cut in under it, sliding the blade away from you as you push. A chocolate curl will roll up onto the blade. Use these large curls to decorate the tops of cakes. Small curls and shavings are made by peeling the side of a room temperature block of chocolate with a standard vegetable peeler. As you peel, hold the chocolate in wax paper or plastic wrap so it won't melt in your hand. Handle the finished curls with a spatula.

CHOCOLATE BAGS

A chocolate bag filled with dipped strawberries is a novel and attractive centerpiece for the dinner table. To make one, paint three layers of chocolate onto the *inside* of a paper bag. When the chocolate has set up you just cut and peel the paper away. Now, because chocolate will take on the finish or shine of whatever surface it is painted onto, a matte (dull gloss) finish will characterize any chocolate bag you create with a paper bag. For a bag with a high gloss, use a plastic lined bag or even a plastic freezer bag. The plastic bag is structurally weak and will collapse when painted with the first coat. While still wet, prop the plastic bag open with crumpled parchment paper or foil. Allow the first layer to set up then pull the crumpled paper out. Some chocolate will break away where the paper was in contact with the real bag. Just paint over these spots and let them harden before applying the second coat. As you paint the inside of the bag, be sure to brush *over*, not into, the seams of the real bag and do give the corners and edges an extra coat for strength. Handle the finished bag carefully. Use plastic wrap between your hands and the chocolate to prevent smudges and finger prints from appearing on its surface.

CHOCOLATE WRITING & DRAWING

Small chocolate letters and numbers can be used to decorate birthday cakes. Hearts, diamonds, triangles, curlicues, birds in flight, Christmas trees, well, anything you can write or draw can also be drawn with chocolate and used as a garnish for desserts. Half fill a paper

Chocolate makes beautiful and edible containers for fruit, mousse and ice cream.

pastry bag with cool but still fluid chocolate. Don't use a metal tip; it will harden the chocolate. Simply adjust the opening to size of a nail hole as you make the bag. Wrap a cutting board with a layer of wax paper or plastic wrap, and, with the chocolate, draw your designs onto the paper. When set, peel paper off the chocolate. This technique also enables you to trace a photograph or other image in chocolate. Just lay the photo or drawing under the paper first, then trace onto plastic or wax paper. These drawings can then be laid onto cakes to give them a very personal touch. If tracing a complex design, remember to connect the lines of your chocolate image so it will be in one piece.

CHOCOLATE CUPS

With a small pastry brush paint a smooth coat of chocolate on the inside of a paper or foil cupcake case. Place the painted case(s) in muffin cups to harden, about 3 minutes in the refrigerator is enough. Apply a second coat and let it set up. Peel paper away from chocolate. Use the cups for serving berries or mousse.

CHOCOLATE COLLAR FOR CAKES

Lay a sheet of parchment paper flat. (Or substitute foil, shiny side up.) The paper must be 1/2 inch longer than the cake is round. Spread a layer of chocolate across the paper, again as thick as a nickel and as wide as you want the collar to be high. Let the chocolate just begin to firm up. Its surface should still be wet. Lift the paper up by its sides, holding it tight. Wrap it around the cake so chocolate covers sides. Hold collar in place for another 2 minutes. When hard, peel paper off the chocolate. Use a warm table knife to weld ends of collar smooth.

CHOCOLATE SHELLS

Cover back of a natural scallop shell (available in gourmet cookware stoes) with plastic wrap. Bunch excess wrap into the hollow in the inside of the shell. Now, wrap back of shell with heavy duty foil, shiny side out. Tuck excess foil into the inside curve of the shell. Rub the foil tightly onto the back of the shell, smoothing out as many wrinkles as possible. Paint three layers onto the back of the shell allowing each layer to dry between coats. Avoid painting over the edge of the foiled shell but do apply chocolate right to the edge. When hard, peel bunched foil back to edge of the shell. Grasp bunched plastic wrap and ift the natural shell out. Now peel foil away from the chocolate shell. Serve berries mousse or mints in these chocolate shells.

CHOCOLATE LEAVES

Chocolate leaves are an elegant addition to cakes and individual desserts. To make a chocolate leaf, paint 2 layers of chocolate onto the *back* of a real leaf. When the chocolate is hard, peel the natural leaf off the chocolate leaf. Sounds simple and it is. Citrus leaves work best. Camellia and ivy leaves are also recommended. Avoid highly toxic plants (just about any plant with white juice) and also avoid leaves with hairy backs; chocolate will stick to them. Be sure to paint right out to the edge of the real leaf but don't paint over the edge; you'll trap the real leaf in the chocolate if you do.

CHOCOLATE FLOWERS

These are exquisite cake decorations. Draw a few stems, paint a few leaves and assemble some chocolate flowers. When you have these on hand you can make an elegant chocolate floral arrangement any time you like.

The flowers are made from a chocolate taffy. This taffy is something many cooks find practical to make out of their leftover, but still liquid, tempered chocolate. It lasts for months. To make it, pour your leftover chocolate into a measuring cup. For every ounce of chocolate add 3/4 tablespoon light corn syrup. That is 3 tablespoons syrup for every 4 ounces chocolate. Stir the syrup and chocolate together until it thickens into a shiny mass that tends to pull away from the spoon. Spread this rather soft taffy onto some plastic wrap, cover it with another sheet of plastic wrap and let it sit for an hour in a cool place.

To make a flower, roll up as many balls of stiff taffy as you want petals in the flower. Vary their size ranging from the equivalent of a teaspoon to a tablespoon. Each ball is then flattened by striking it with the flat side of a chef's knife or metal spatula. As you strike the ball, slide the knife away from you so it polishes the flattening surface. After ten strikes the ball should be a flat disk, and its far edge should be quite thin. This is the petal. Free it from the work surface by setting the cutting edge of your blade just under the thicker side of the petal, then swiftly pass the knife under the petal. Roll this first petal into a cylinder with the thin edge on top. Continue making petals. Add new petals to the flower as you make them. Simply wrap their thicker sides around the bottom of the forming flower allowing the thinner, more delicate edges to bend out from the center. As you work keep the flower's base pinched against the side of your cutting board. Don't let it rest on its side; the petals are still too soft for the flower to be laid on its side. It will stiffen up after 10 minutes. The taffy can be touched without melting so use your fingertips to pinch and bend the outer edges of the petals to shape the flower to your taste.

You can also use the taffy to make ribbons that can be tied into bows around desserts such as poached pears and petits fours. To do so, pass the taffy through the rollers of a pasta machine set for medium thickness. This will produce a sheet of chocolate taffy. Cut the sheet into ribbons with a circular pizza knife or simply pass it through the noodle cutting rollers on your pasta machine.

Aspic & Chaud-Froid

Today only professional chefs working in exclusive clubs and resorts are given the time to make center pieces of large cold roasts and fish. Their traditional approach is to coat these cooked foods in sauces and stocks to which gelatin has been added, called *chaud-froid*. A first coat is typically an opaque white sauce such as bechamel, although brown sauce is also used. This chaud-froid will harden because of the gelatin and serve as a canvas on which the chef will then arrrange a mosaic of thin pieces of food. The mosaic is then covered with a clear layer of gelatinized stock called aspic. The aspic seals the design and the chaud-froid giving the centerpiece a glistening luster.

Chaud-froid means hot-cold, a simple French term to describe a sauce that is prepared hot but served cold. It is pronounced *show-fwah*. Coating and decorating a three dimensional object such as a turkey or salmon is a feat requiring a large refrigerator (the walk-in size is the most practical) and enormous amounts of sauces and stocks. Thankfully, the process also lends itself to decorating serving platters and this is quicker, more economical and manageable for all cooks. These decorated trays are then used to present hors-d'oeuvres and cold buffet items. As the food on the tray is eaten the tray keeps its attractive design.

The simplest coating process is that of pouring a 1/4-inch-deep layer of clear amber aspic onto the tray and allowing it to harden. Cold foods are laid onto the surface of the aspic and never come into contact with the metal tray, which might taint their delicate flavors.

WHITE CHAUD-FROID

The full, three layer process begins with a recipe for white chaud-froid:

1. Pour 1 cup of tap water into a soup bowl. Sprinkle with 4 tablespoons plain gelatin powder. Let the gelatin soften and absorb the water.

2. Meanwhile, scald 3 cups whole milk.

3. Melt 2 tablespoons of shortening in a 2-quart saucepan. When it is just melted, add 4 tablespoons all-purpose flour; stir the mixture until it bubbles and foams. Do not brown.

4. Add hot milk; whisk over a medium-high heat until mixture boils. Do not let this burn or the sauce will have brown spots in it. Let the sauce cool for a few minutes. Stir in the softened gelatin. Once the gelatin is well blended with the white sauce, pour through a very fine strainer into a second pan.

5. Cool the sauce by placing the pot in an ice water bath in the sink. Slowly stir it while it cools. When cool, pour it onto the trays, but just enough to coat the surface.

Before going on, please note that this recipe is absolutely tasteless and is intended as a decorative tray undercoating. If you want to serve chaud-froid coated foods, cut the gelatin in half and substitute half of the milk with a well flavored stock. Also realize that you will need to apply two or three layers to the foods so they will have a decent coating. To do this efficiently, have the foods resting on a fine-meshed cake rack which in turn, is resting on a cookie sheet or shallow baking pan. Each layer must be allowed to cool and harden before applying the next.

To decorate the tray (or food) select components of your mosaic for their colors. Suggestions are: wilted green onion and leek leaves, strips or sheets of wilted carrot slices, lemon, orange, or lime peel, red radishes and grapes, ripe and green olives and pimiento

strips. Wilt items in boiling water that curl. Do not use fresh pineapple or kiwifruit.

All the foods must be thinly sliced. Clear aspic must cover the mosaic and seal it completely. If the foods are thicker than a nickel, the clear coat will be too dense.

Assemble the mosaic on a cutting board to be sure it is what you want. If you are gifted as an artist, your design may be full of intricate details and fine lines. Most cooks, however, are advised to keep their first few designs rather simple—a few flowers, for instance. Use green onion leaves for stems and leaves. Cut the flower petals from carrot strips, red radishes, zucchini, olives and grapes—either rounds or ovals. You may want to make an arrangement of flowers, then weave a basket at their base. Create a bunch of grapes and a wine glass, or a fish with scales of cucumber slices. If you have a set of aspic cutters, use them to punch hearts, diamonds, teardrops and circles. Arrange these in a simple border around edge of the tray.

Once the design is cut and ready to apply, dissolve 1-1/2 tablespoons powdered gelatin powder in 2 cups tap water. Let it soften, then heat it until it clears. Stir it slowly while it heats; gelatin burns very easily. Once cleared, chill it in an ice bath—again, stirring very slowly. Remove the coated tray from refrigerator. Dip each piece of your design into the cold but still liquid gelatin and place them, one at a time, on the cold tray. When finished, return the tray to the refrigerator to harden.

When set, pour the remaining clear gelatin over the mosaic.

Ice Carving

Ice carvings are far easier to sculpt than their delicate elegance suggests. To create your own frozen sculpture, begin with a look at the practical limits of your situation. How large is

your freezer? Where are you going to do the carving? How well do you sculpt? How much time do you have and what tools do you need?

Fortunately, you don't have to be an

accomplished sculptor in order to carve an attractive ice sculpture. Ice is suprisingly easy to saw, chip and chisel. Ice is quite soft, and few are the carvings that take more than two hours to complete. Ten and twenty pound blocks of beautiful clear ice are available at supermarkets. These smaller blocks are more practical than the 300 pound blocks used by professional chefs. Few kitchens have the walk-in freezer required to store these large blocks which are 40 inches high, 20 inches wide and 10 inches thick.

What about your sculptural ability? If the idea of carving a swan is too scary at first, begin with a design you can manage. A flower vase or basket is a wonderful start. Make it a plain urn shape or add one or two handles. Design a hollow in its top so you can set a block of green florist's foam (called Oasis) into the hollow. Place an arrangement of vegetable flowers or real flowers in the foam. Simple structures such as a classical arch or a pyramid or the Eiffel Tower are other good beginnings. A Christmas tree, a star, crescent moon or burning candle are more examples of clean designs suitable for beginning ice carvers.

Plan to work outdoors where it doesn't matter if the ground gets wet. Obviously, pick a shady spot. The temperature can be as warm as 70 degrees Fahrenheit (20C). The lower the humidity the better. Under these conditions you'll have up to two hours to complete the carving. If you aren't finished by then, refreeze the piece and begin again in a few hours. Always set the ice block on towels so it won't slip around, and use a very sturdy stand or table.

The tools you need are:

1.   A saw with fairly long, large teeth. A chain saw works very well and saves lots of time. Be sure any electrical equipment used is double insulated and grounded. Some ice sculptors also use an electric grinder fitted with a wire brush, which cuts through ice very smoothly.

2.   An ice chipper. This hand tool looks like an oversize fork. It has six or more tines, each shaped like a thick ice pick. Ice picks themselves cause deep cracks through the ice.

3.   A set of flat chisels suitable for wood carving, ranging in width from one to three inches. Curved chisels may come in handy.

4.   Safety goggles and insulated rubber gloves are also necessary. Have a few old towels and a stiff brush to wipe your sculpture off with, too.

Start the carving process by sketching your design on paper. Draw a front view and the views from both the right and left sides exactly the same size as the carving. As you plan the design, leave the bottom 15 percent of the ice block as is. The carving needs this weight and mass at its bottom for stability. Cut your sketches out. The first step with the ice is to trace the silhouette of each view into the ice.

Take the ice out of the freezer and set it in position. Ice needs to warm up to reduce its tendency to crack. Twenty-eight degrees Fahrenheit is the optimum ice temperature. A good rule of thumb is to wait for the frosty surface to clear before cutting into the block. Hold your paper patterns in place and scratch their outlines into the ice with the edge of the chipper or electric grinder.

Block-cut the large areas away with the saw, working as close to the design as possible. Use the chipper and chisels to carve the finished form. Wait until last to carve details into the design and, when you do, cut all details at least 1/2 inch deep into the surfaces.

As you go about the carving, never strike the ice hard with any tool. Use a repetition of soft, short, shaving strokes. Also, never chip or chisel across a corner. Face the cutting edge of the tool directly into a corner aiming at the interior of the block, otherwise the corner breaks off. One more cautionary note: don't use hammers or mallets alone or together with the chisels or chipper. If a large piece of ice mistakenly breaks off during the carving, you'll have to alter your design accordingly or start over.

Patterns

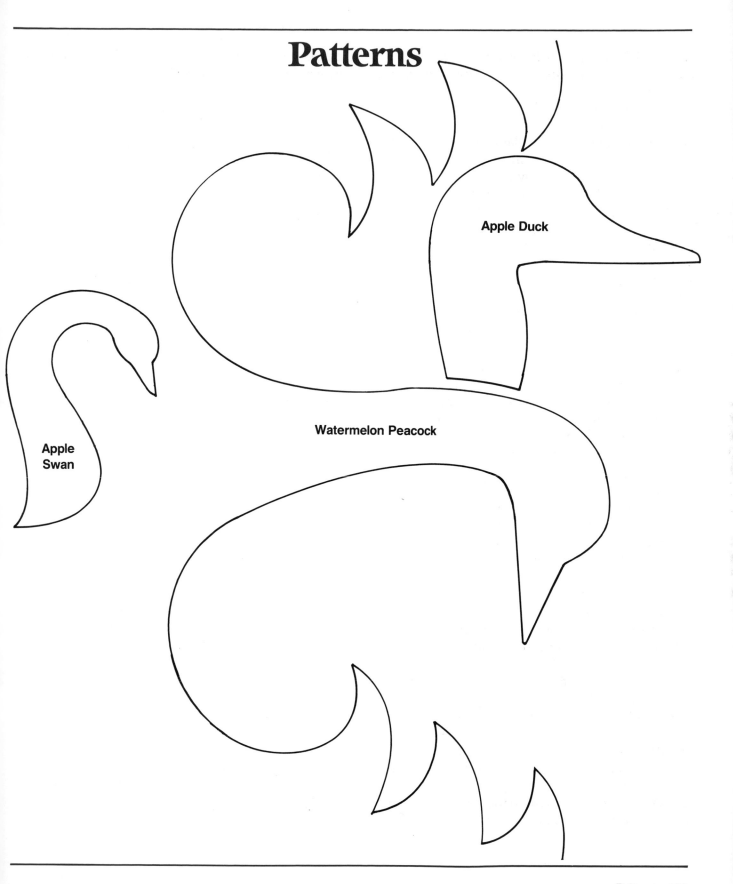

Apple Duck

Apple
Swan

Watermelon Peacock

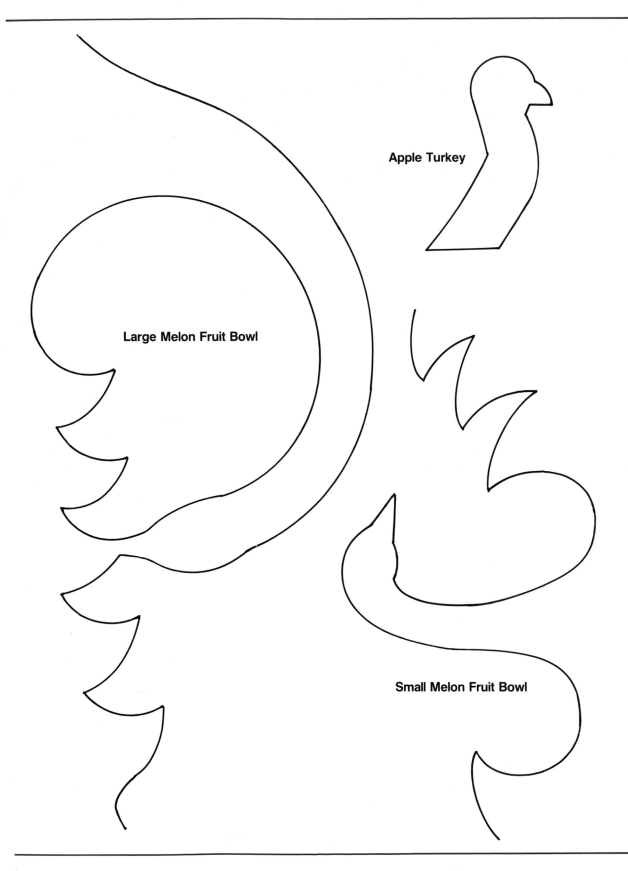

Apple Turkey

Large Melon Fruit Bowl

Small Melon Fruit Bowl

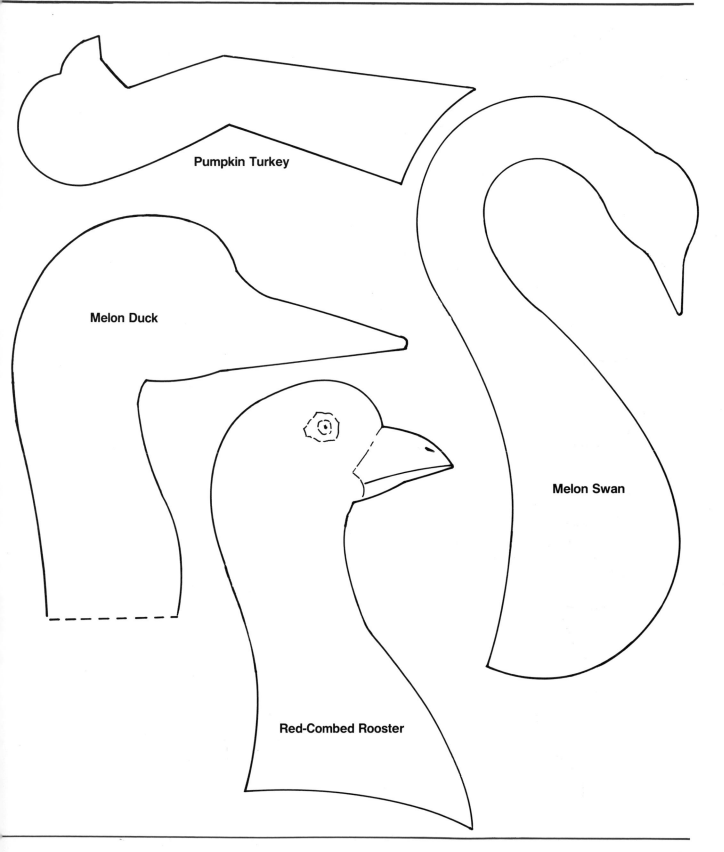

Pumpkin Turkey

Melon Duck

Melon Swan

Red-Combed Rooster

Index

Metric Chart

Comparison to Metric Measure

When You Know	Symbol	Multiply By	To Find	Symbol
teaspoons	tsp	5.0	milliliters	ml
tablespoons	tbsp	15.0	milliliters	ml
fluid ounces	fl. oz.	30.0	milliliters	ml
cups	c	0.24	liters	l
pints	pt.	0.47	liters	l
quarts	qt.	0.95	liters	l
ounces	oz.	28.0	grams	g
pounds	lb.	0.45	kilograms	kg
Fahrenheit	F	5/9 (after subtracting 32)	Celsius	C

Fahrenheit to Celsius

F	C
200—205	95
220—225	105
245—250	120
275	135
300—305	150
325—330	165
345—350	175
370—375	190
400—405	205
425—430	220
445—450	230
470—475	245
500	260

Liquid Measure to Liters

1/4 cup	=	0.06 liters
1/2 cup	=	0.12 liters
3/4 cup	=	0.18 liters
1 cup	=	0.24 liters
1-1/4 cups	=	0.3 liters
1-1/2 cups	=	0.36 liters
2 cups	=	0.48 liters
2-1/2 cups	=	0.6 liters
3 cups	=	0.72 liters
3-1/2 cups	=	0.84 liters
4 cups	=	0.96 liters
4-1/2 cups	=	1.08 liters

Liquid Measure to Milliliters

1/4 teaspoon	=	1.25 milliliters
1/2 teaspoon	=	2.5 milliliters
3/4 teaspoon	=	3.75 milliliters
1 teaspoon	=	5.0 milliliters
1-1/4 teaspoons	=	6.25 milliliters
1-1/2 teaspoons	=	7.5 milliliters
1-3/4 teaspoons	=	8.75 milliliters
2 teaspoons	=	10.0 milliliters
1 tablespoon	=	15.0 milliliters
2 tablespoons	=	30.0 milliliters